12 Genre Mini-Books

by Betsy Franco

NONFICTION — **All About Spiders**

PLAY — **A Pollution Solution**

BIOGRAPHY — **Jane Goodall and the Chimps**

HISTORICAL FICT — **Escape in the Night**

POETRY — **All Sorts of Animal Poems**

HUMOROUS FICTION — **Backwards Viv**

ADVENTURE — **Lost in the Snow**

MYSTERY — **The Mystery of the Missing Cat Food**

REALISTIC FICTION — **The Big Race**

SCIENCE FICTION/FANTASY — **Space Scooters on Mars**

FAIRY TALE — **Tom Thumb**

TALL TALE — **Paul Bunyan and Babe the Blue Ox**

SCHOLASTIC

PROFESSIONAL BOOKS

New York • Toronto • London • Auckland • Sydney
Mexico City • New Delhi • Hong Kong • Buenos Aires

Dedication

For Liza Charlesworth, whose great ideas
always stretch my writing

Special thanks to Katy Obringer,
an extraordinary librarian at the Palo Alto
Children's Library, who helped me
with the "Booklinks"

Acknowledgments

"Habitats" from *Poem of the Week*, Book 3. © 2000 by Betsy Franco.
Used by permission of the author.

"Buffalo" from *What If? Just Wondering Poems* by Joy N. Hulme.
Copyright © 1993 by Joy N. Hulme. Used by permission of the author.

"Rhinocerecess" by Leslie Danford Perkins. Copyright © 1996
by Leslie Danford Perkins. Used by permission of the author.

Cover design by Kelli Thompson
Cover artwork by Julie Durrell, Patrick Girouard, and Jenny Williams
Interior design by Sydney Wright
Interior artwork by Julie Durrell, Patrick Girouard, Mike Moran, George Ulrich,
Jenny Williams, and Patricia Wynne

ISBN: 0-439-30962-X
Copyright © 2002 by Betsy Franco
All rights reserved. Published by Scholastic Inc.
Printed in the U.S.A.

Contents

Introduction

Bring literary genres alive for students at the primary level! *12 Genre Mini-Books* puts 12 mini-books into the hands of every child in your class and leapfrogs them into enjoying broader reading and writing experiences.

Young learners can have exciting experience with different types of genres. And as an integral part of the National Council of Teachers of English (NCTE) reading and writing standards, they're as important as ever to share with students. Until now, age-appropriate materials have not been readily accessible for teaching genre to younger children.

Now with *12 Genre Mini-Books*, you don't have to worry about collecting books from each genre and trying to provide multiple copies for the children in your class. In this wonderful collection, each child has his or her own personal library of mini-books, each one tailor-made to delight primary readers.

Every genre unit includes not only the mini-books but also instant activities to reinforce the distinctive elements of the genre. Once children have been guided to discover the attributes of each genre, they can create a class web to deepen their understanding. There are also 12 writing prompts to enable children to have firsthand experience with each literary genre.

Booklinks supplement each unit by offering lists of age-appropriate books in the same genres. You can read them to the class, or you can make them available in class for children to expand their reading horizons.

Making the Most of Genre Mini-Books

This collection has been designed for maximum flexibility. You can use the mini-books in the order they appear, find the genre you are currently studying, or use a genre that relates to a theme or unit you are working on. For example, the Jane Goodall biography would weave nicely into a unit on animals, *The Big Race* would work well in a values unit about good sportsmanship or friendship.

As you begin teaching each unit, talk about the genre with your students. You'll learn what they already know and where their interests lie. Then consider the following teaching sequence:

1. Ask your students to bring in favorite books from home. If you're studying fairy tales, your students' home libraries will be treasure troves of examples. For many students the concept of genre may be unfamiliar, so providing them with concrete examples through stories they know is a helpful way to support their learning.

2. Invite your students to assemble and color their very own genre mini-books. Read the book as a shared reading activity. Or, if you prefer, invite students to read it on their own, with a partner, or in small groups.

3. Provide each of your students with a copy of the activity page that goes with the story they've just read. Each Activity Page asks students to:

● identify key information regarding the story, such as characters and setting.

Building Skills

Teaching with the genre mini-books in this collection helps children learn to:

✦ recognize and identify different genres and understand the differences between them.

✦ appreciate and look for specific elements of a genre when reading books.

✦ use the mini-books as models for creative writing in the style of a particular genre.

✦ stretch their own writing styles and reading interests.

Story Map

Name _____

Directions: Fill in this story map to organize your ideas before you begin writing.

Who or what is it about?
Characters: _____
Topic: _____

What's the setting?
Time: _____
Place: _____

What's the genre?
Story title: _____

What happens in the story?
Beginning: _____
Middle: _____
End: _____

How else will your writing fit the genre?

Is there a main problem?
Explain: _____
How is it solved: _____

Name _____

Genre Web

Directions: Complete the web below. Use your mini-book to think about this genre.

Characters

Are they real or pretend? Explain. _____

Setting

Does the story take place now, the future, or in the past? Explain. _____

Is the setting important? Why? _____

What's the genre?

Main Problem

Could the problem really happen? Explain. _____

Could the solution really happen? Explain. _____

What else do you know about this genre?

● classify the elements in each story that are integral to that particular genre.

● write within a particular genre by using the writing prompts and the Story Map reproducible on page 84.

4. Give each of your students a copy of the Genre Web template on page 83. Then as a class have them:

● write the name of the genre in the center rectangle of the web.

● use each mini-book to identify the elements particular to each genre (in general).

● record each characteristic in the boxes that extend from the center rectangle.

5. Introduce additional literature for your students to read as a class or on their own. The Booklinks found on page 85-86 are organized by genre and includes books that are sure to be a hit with your students.

6. Encourage your students to take home the Genre Mini-Books they've read to share with family members and friends. Before they know it, your students' home libraries will include a whole collection of mini-books that span the genres.

Assembling the Mini-Books

Begin by making copies of the mini-book you would like to use. Keeping the pages faceup, invert every other page. Place the pages in your photocopier and make one double-sided copy of the mini-book for each student.

By constructing a few genre mini-books as a class activity, your students are sure to enjoy making them on their own and reading the mini-books they've created. Introduce the bookmaking process by showing your students what they'll be expected to do—from folding and matching up the pages to stapling and coloring. Demonstrate and discuss each of the steps.

TIP!

For younger students you may find it helpful to assemble the books in advance, especially at the beginning of the school year. With time, they'll become adept at making books independently.

1. Put the pages in order. For an 7-page book, place page B faceup on top of page A.

For a 11-page book, place page B faceup on top of page A. Then place page C faceup on top of page B.

2. Fold the pages in half along the dotted line, making a little book.

3. Check to be sure that all of the pages are in sequence. Then, staple them together along the book's spine.

4. Once the mini-book is assembled, it's time to invite your students to color the pictures and read the mini-book!

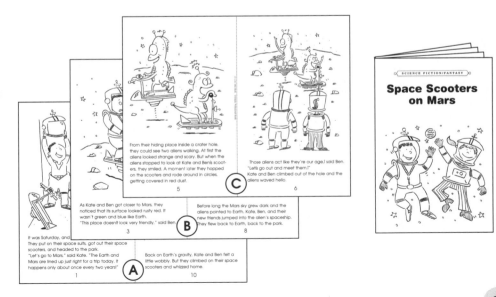

All About Spiders

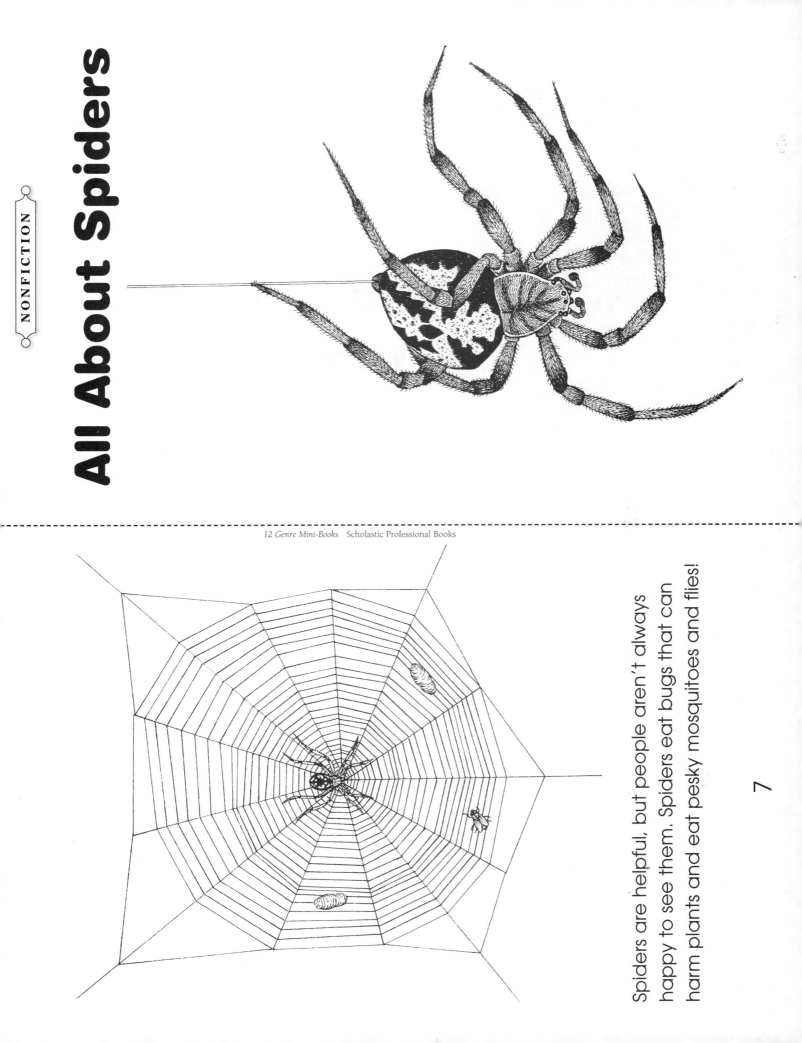

Spiders are helpful, but people aren't always happy to see them. Spiders eat bugs that can harm plants and eat pesky mosquitoes and flies!

7

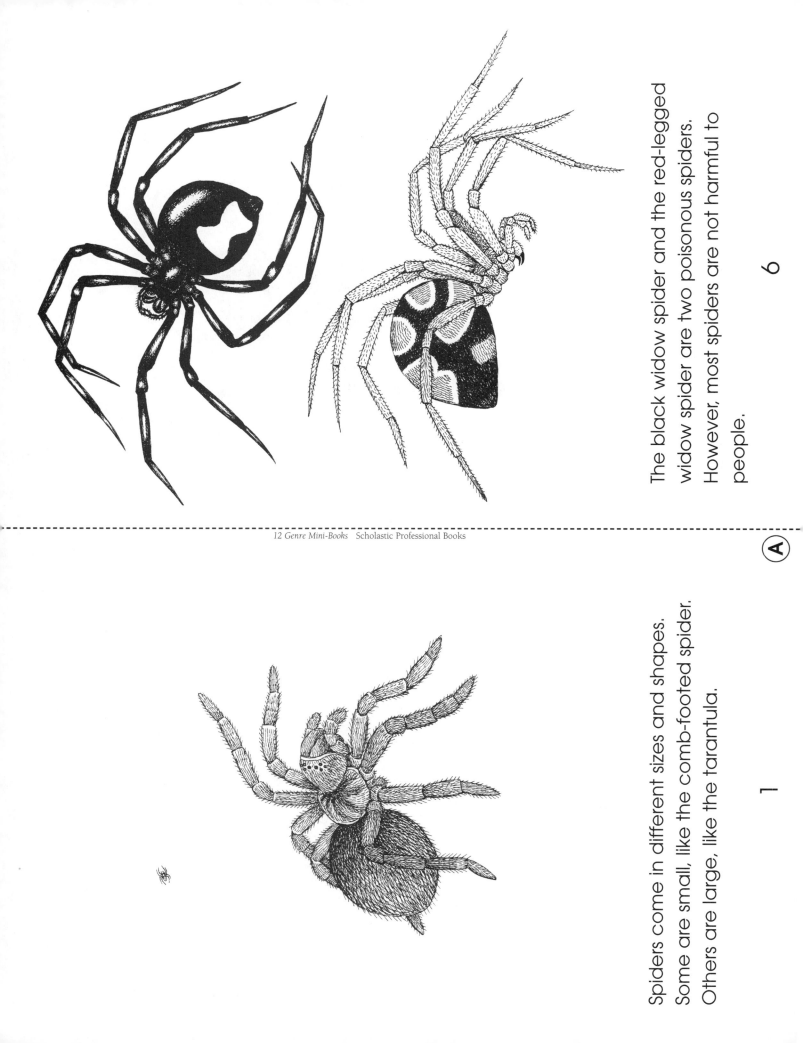

The black widow spider and the red-legged widow spider are two poisonous spiders. However, most spiders are not harmful to people.

6

Ⓐ

Spiders come in different sizes and shapes. Some are small, like the comb-footed spider. Others are large, like the tarantula.

1

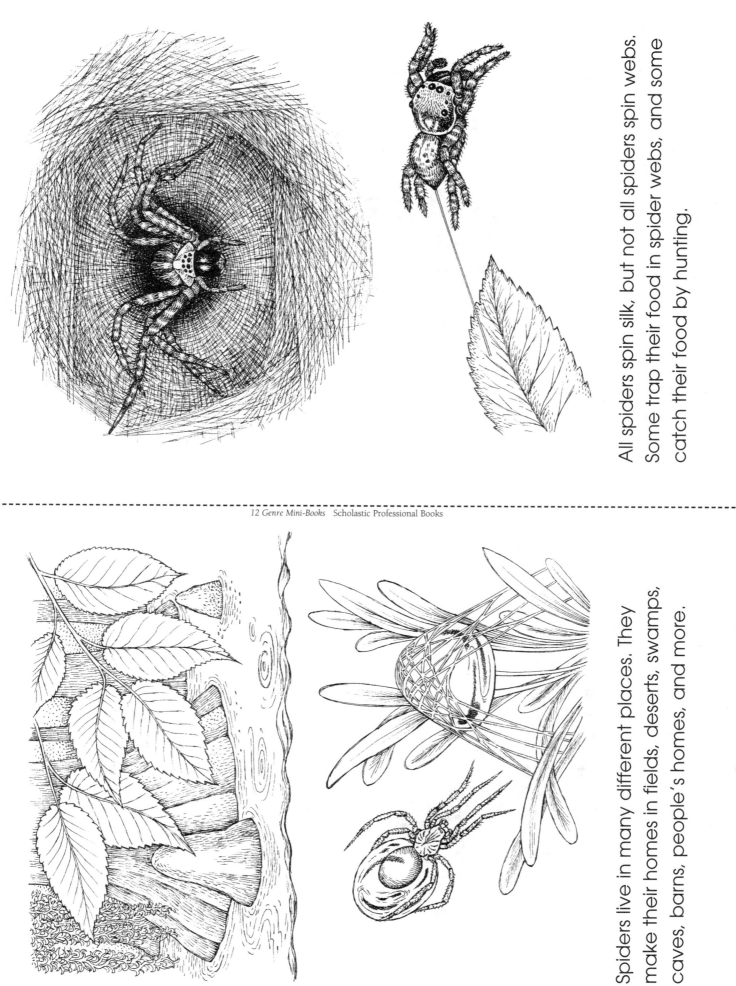

All spiders spin silk, but not all spiders spin webs. Some trap their food in spider webs, and some catch their food by hunting.

4

Ⓑ

Spiders live in many different places. They make their homes in fields, deserts, swamps, caves, barns, people's homes, and more.

3

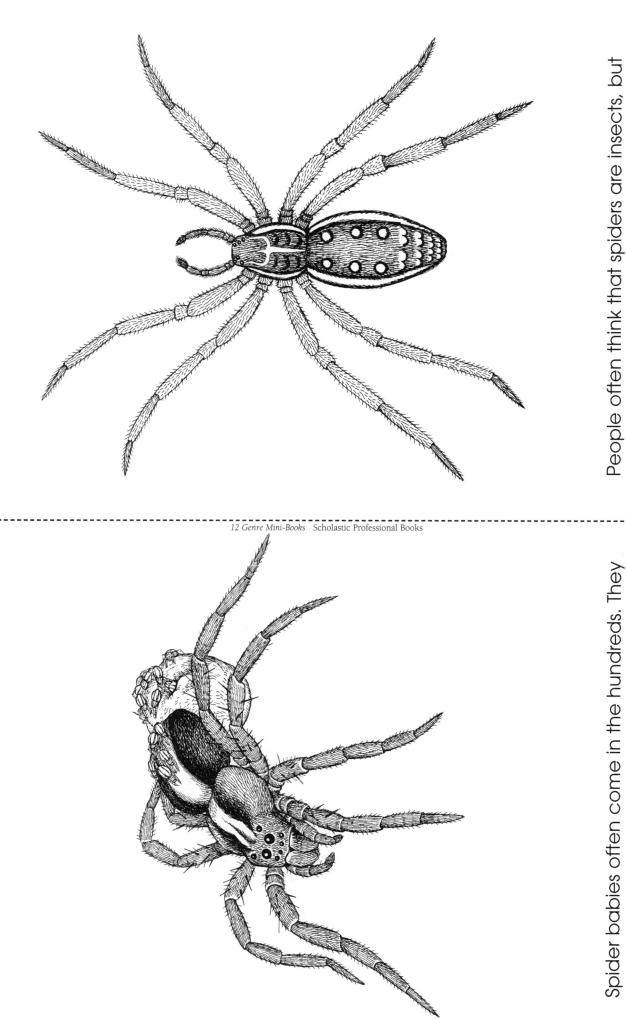

People often think that spiders are insects, but they aren't. Insects have six legs and spiders have eight.

2

Spider babies often come in the hundreds. They hatch out of little eggs inside of an egg sac. When it's warm outside, the spiderlings make a hole in the sac and climb out, one at a time.

5

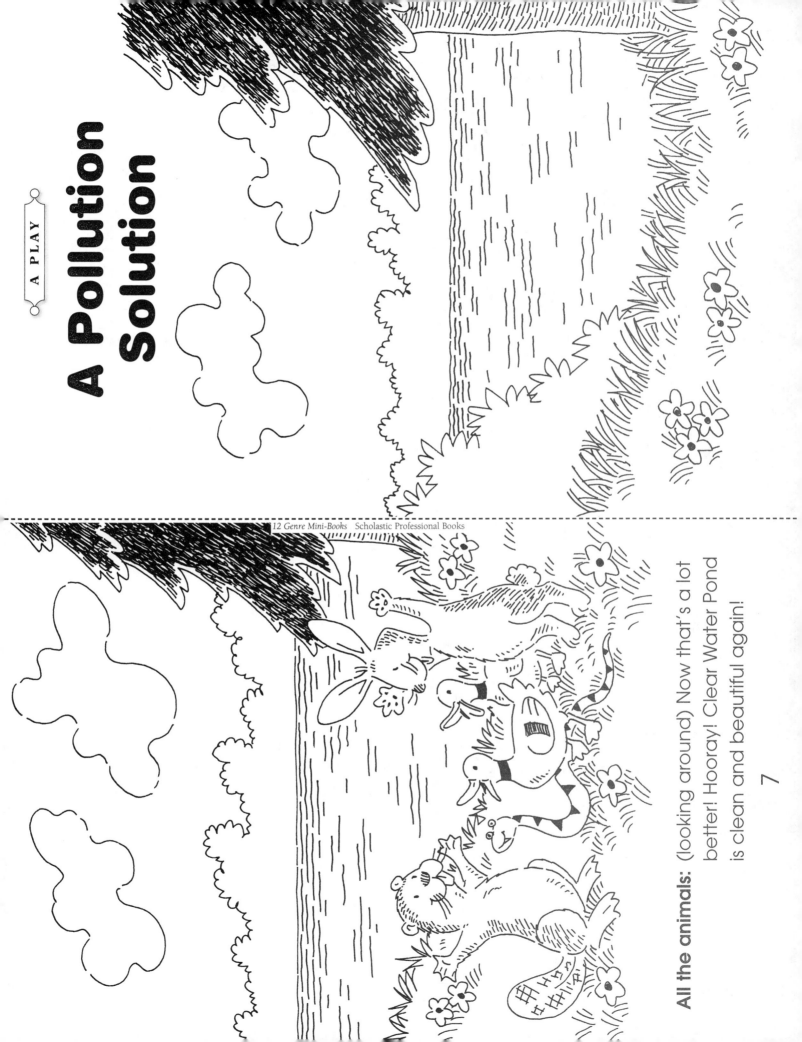

A Pollution Solution

All the animals: (looking around) Now that's a lot better! Hooray! Clear Water Pond is clean and beautiful again!

7

Narrator: That day, Mr. Berger's second and third graders picked up all the bottles, cans, papers, and garbage they could find at Clear Water Pond. They placed all of it in containers to be recycled.

6

Ⓐ

Setting:
Clear Water Pond

Characters:
Narrator
Beaver
Snake
Rabbit
Duck
Mr. Berger, the teacher
Students

Optional props:
cans
papers
plastic bottle
paper plates

1

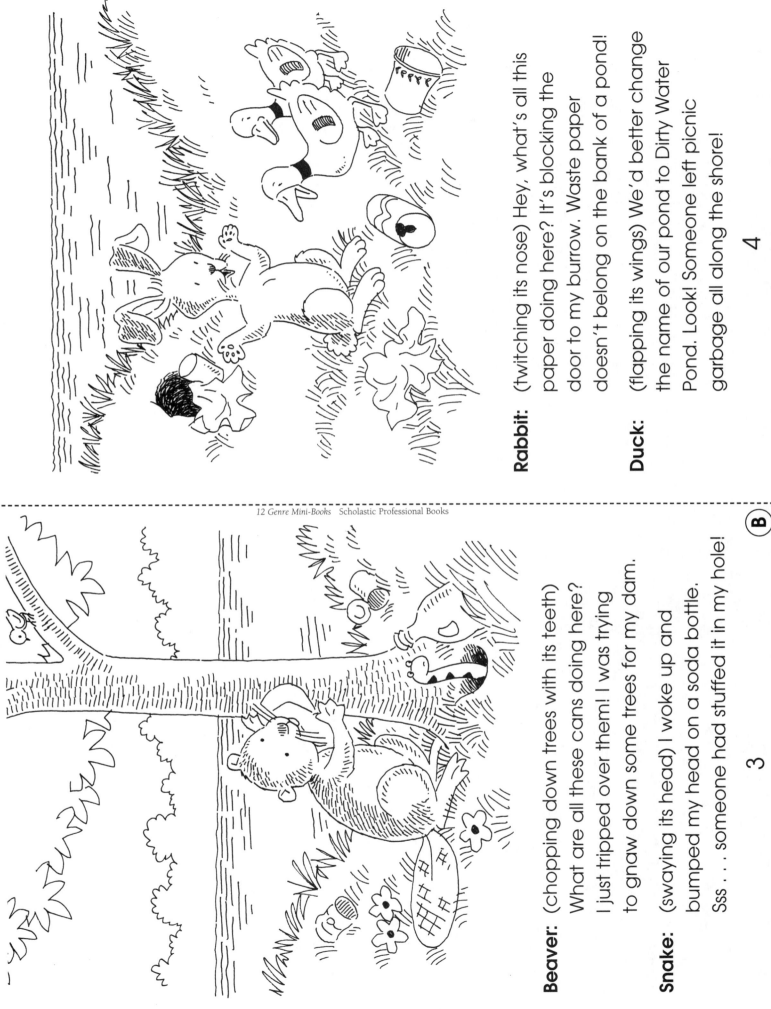

Rabbit: (twitching its nose) Hey, what's all this paper doing here? It's blocking the door to my burrow. Waste paper doesn't belong on the bank of a pond!

Duck: (flapping its wings) We'd better change the name of our pond to Dirty Water Pond. Look! Someone left picnic garbage all along the shore!

4

12 *Genre Mini-Books* Scholastic Professional Books

Beaver: (chopping down trees with its teeth) What are all these cans doing here? I just tripped over them! I was trying to gnaw down some trees for my dam.

Snake: (swaying its head) I woke up and bumped my head on a soda bottle. Sss . . . someone had stuffed it in my hole!

3

Ⓑ

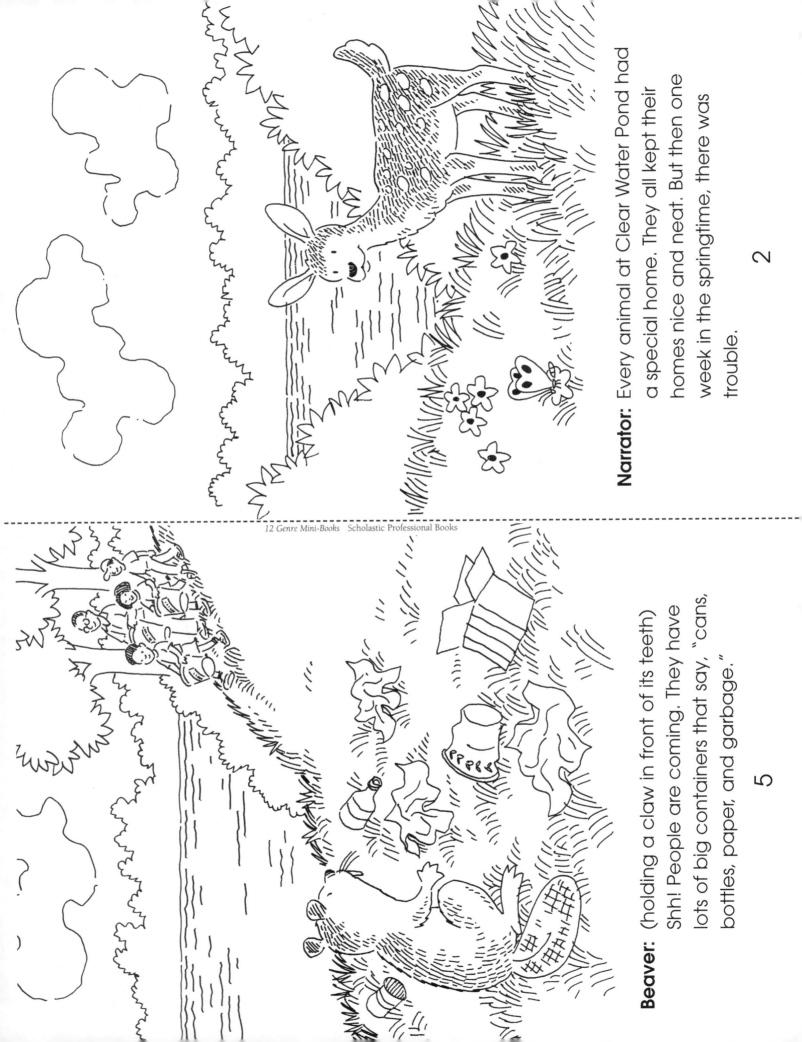

Narrator: Every animal at Clear Water Pond had a special home. They all kept their homes nice and neat. But then one week in the springtime, there was trouble.

2

Beaver: (holding a claw in front of its teeth) Shh! People are coming. They have lots of big containers that say, "cans, bottles, paper, and garbage."

5

Jane Goodall and the Chimps

Whenever she can, Jane returns to Africa to be with the chimps. She also writes books and gives talks. She wants to help people understand why it is so important to take care of wild animals and the habitats in which they live.

11

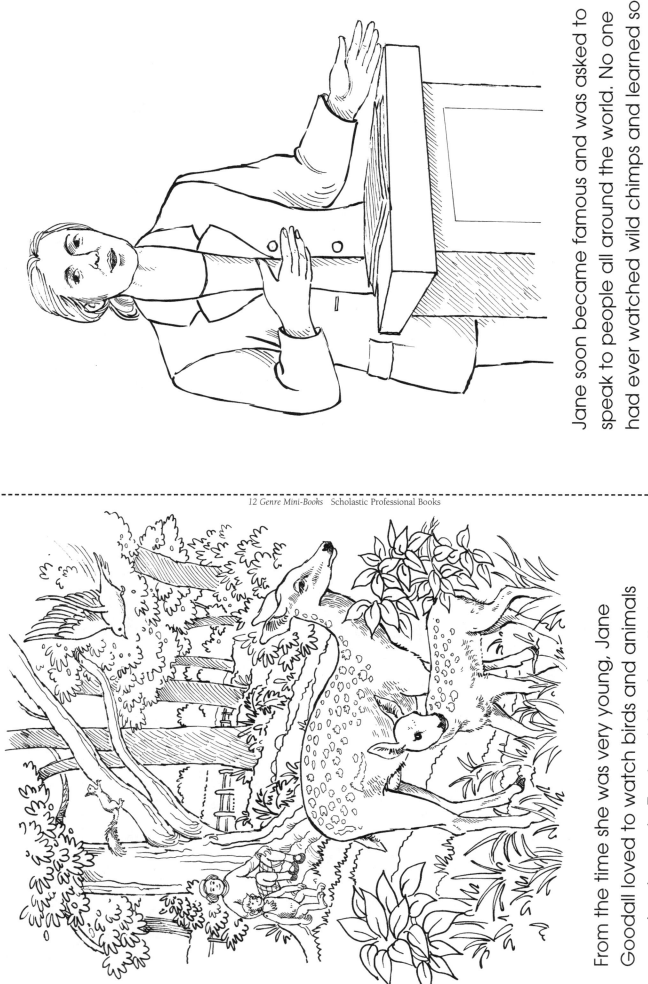

Jane soon became famous and was asked to speak to people all around the world. No one had ever watched wild chimps and learned so much about them. Jane's knowledge helped scientists understand human beings better.

10

From the time she was very young, Jane Goodall loved to watch birds and animals near her home in England. Her favorite toy was a stuffed chimpanzee named Jubilee.

1

Ⓐ

When Jane was four years old, she sat for hours in the hen house. Later, she told her mother that she had waited and waited and waited there to watch a hen lay an egg.

2

Jane studied how families and groups of chimps got along. She discovered how smart they are when she saw a chimp make a tool. The chimp took the leaves off of a stick. Then it poked the stick in a termite hole and pulled up termites to eat.

9

After five months, the chimps had at last grown used to Jane. David Graybeard was the name of the first chimp to touch her. She held a nut in her hand. He reached for it and held her hand softly.

8

Ⓑ

Jane always wanted to go to Africa where there were lots of wild animals. Then, when she was older, a friend who lived in Africa invited Jane for a visit. Jane worked hard to save money for the trip.

3

In Africa, Jane met a famous scientist named Dr. Louis Leakey. She helped him dig up bones that had been buried for millions of years.

4

Finally, after many months, she saw a group of chimps. From then on she watched them quietly for hours every day. Sometimes she slept near them. Eventually, Jane gave the chimps names like Flo, Fifi, and Mr. McGregor.

7

Jane and her mother lived alone in two small tents in the middle of the jungle. Every day Jane would go looking for chimps.

6

Ⓒ

Dr. Leakey invited Jane to study a group of chimpanzees in Africa. She was thrilled to live with the chimps and study them. She invited her mother to come with her.

5

HISTORICAL FICTION

Escape in the Night

12 *Genre Mini-Books* Scholastic Professional Books

"We're free now for the rest of our lives!"
Tina said.

11

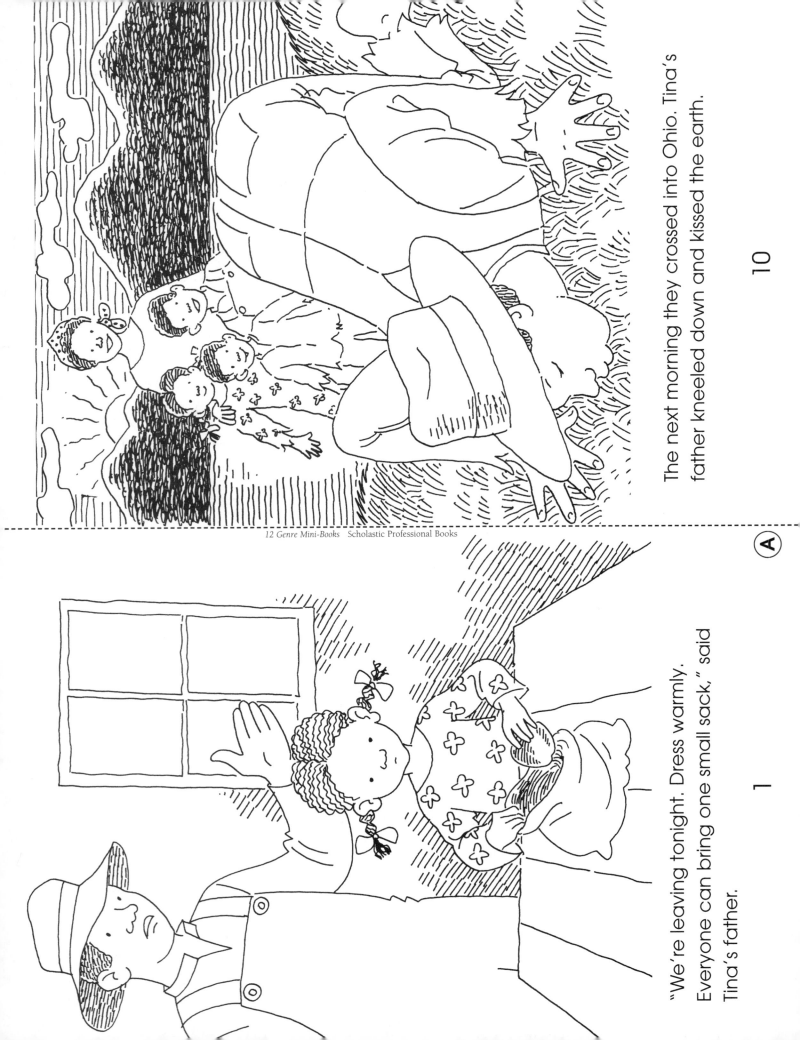

The next morning they crossed into Ohio. Tina's father kneeled down and kissed the earth.

10

Ⓐ

"We're leaving tonight. Dress warmly. Everyone can bring one small sack," said Tina's father.

1

Tina and her family had been slaves for years.
They had been working in the fields for no pay.
And her father had been beaten.

2

"You're close to the free state of Ohio. You won't be slaves there," said one of their helpers. "Be careful," he said as he pointed up the river.

9

When they felt lost, they followed the North Star and the rivers that flowed northward. All along the journey, people in the Underground Railroad hid them and fed them.

8

"I've heard of an underground railroad," said Father. "It's not really a train. It's people in the country and the cities who will help us travel north to freedom. But first, we need to escape from this plantation."

3

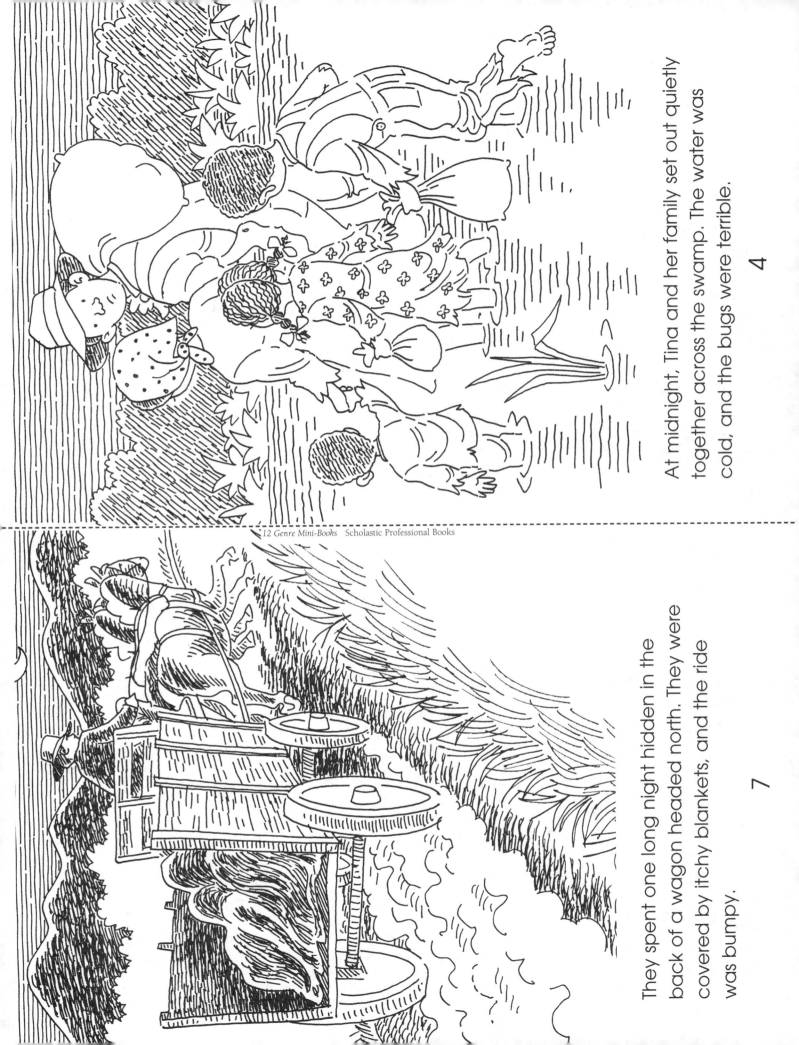

At midnight, Tina and her family set out quietly together across the swamp. The water was cold, and the bugs were terrible.

4

They spent one long night hidden in the back of a wagon headed north. They were covered by itchy blankets, and the ride was bumpy.

7

Every night, the family walked nearly 20 miles. During the day, they hid in churches, caves, and people's homes. Night and day, Tina prayed they wouldn't be discovered.

6

ⓒ

"There's a lantern over there," whispered Tina. "That must be one of our helpers on the Underground Railroad. I was told to look out for lanterns, candles, quilts, and flags," said Father.

5

All Sorts of Animal Poems

Rhinocerecess

On the playground rhinos chase,
In a wild rhinocerace.
Up the ropes and down the slides,
Going for rhinocerides.

In a puddle rhinos stomp,
Having a rhinoceromp.
Muddy rhinos wade in pools,
Breaking the rhinocerules.

Recess ends and rhinos go,
In a neat rhinocerow,
Back to class, where they are quick
To learn rhinocerithmetic.

—*Leslie Danford Perkins*

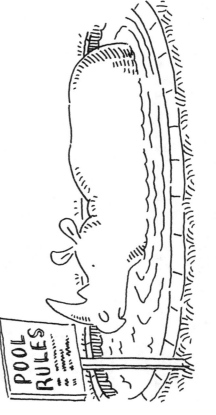

7

The Catfight

yowwwling
grrrowling
flying fur
kicking feet
screeches
scratches
shrieks

Then quiet—
as two tattered cats
slink on home,
looking back over
their shoulders.

—Betsy Franco

6

Ⓐ

Being an Elephant

An elephant
   trumpets
   and drinks
   and bathes
and flaps its giant ears with ease.

It knocks down branches it can eat
by wrapping its trunk around the trees.

Being an elephant would be neat.
if it didn't have such baggy knees!

—Betsy Franco

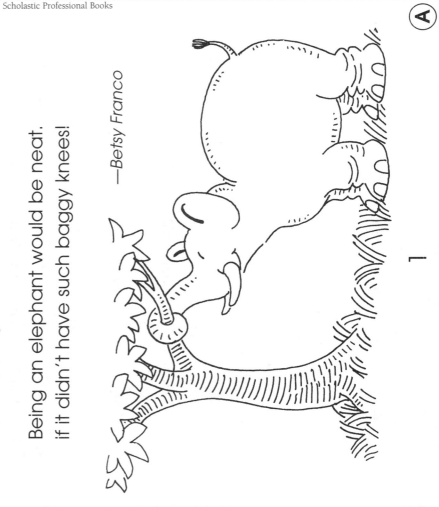

1

Buffalo

Wouldn't it be fun to know
A shaggly, scraggly buffalo
With bearded chin and hairy hide
And hump-shaped back to climb and ride,
With horns like handles on his head?
You'd best beware of him instead.
'Cause buffalo don't like to play.
Their stony stares say, "Stay away."

—Joy N. Hulme

4

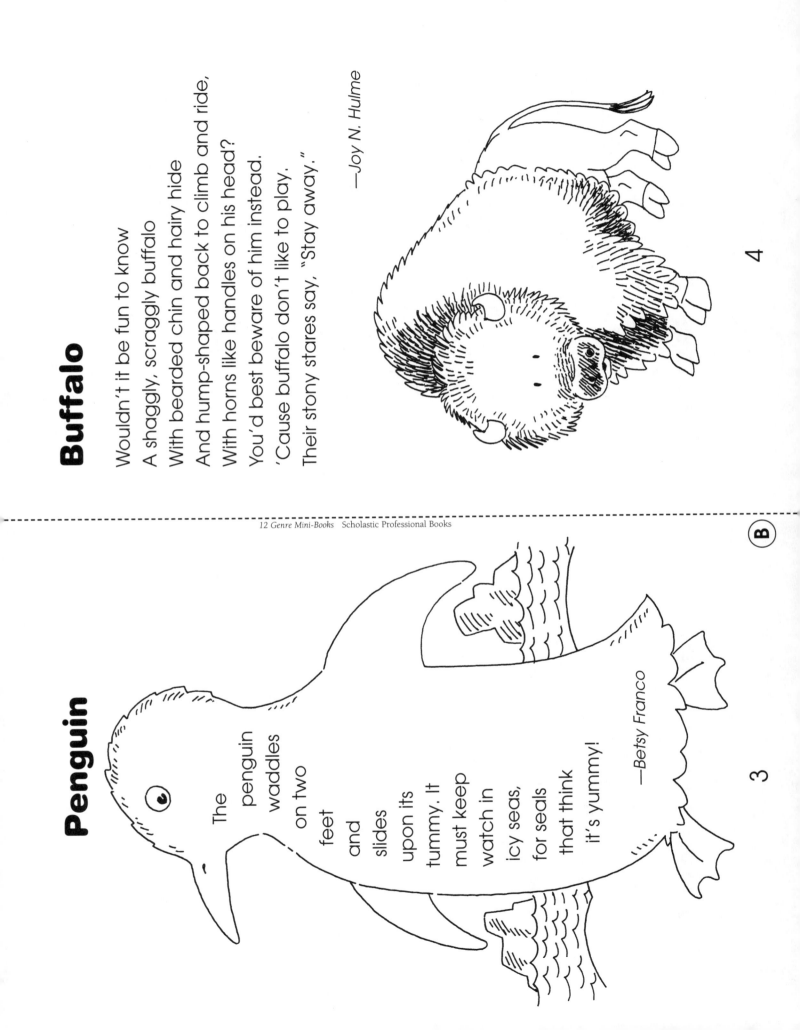

Ⓑ

Penguin

The
penguin
waddles
on two
feet
and
slides
upon its
tummy. It
must keep
watch in
icy seas,
for seals
that think
it's yummy!

—Betsy Franco

3

Habitats

The lizard crawls from under the rocks.
She warms her scales in the morning sun.

The bullfrog camps on the edge of the pond.
He watches and waits for his afternoon meal.

The bat unfolds his giant wings.
He leaves his cave to hunt by the moon.

I throw off the covers and climb out of bed.
I toss a shirt on my bedroom floor.

But unlike the lizard, the frog, and the bat,
my mom makes me clean up my habitat!

—Betsy Franco

2

My Dog is Missing

I miss her wiggle, I miss her wag.
I miss her tail that waves like a flag.
I miss her eyes that beg me to play.
I miss when she sits if I say, "Stay!"
I miss her slobbery tongue on my face.
I miss her balls all over the place.
Hey, who's that stranger at the door?
My dog isn't missing anymore!

—Betsy Franco

5

Backwards Viv

So she called herself Vivian from that day on. The only thing backwards about Vivian was her baseball cap!

7

"Enough is enough," said Viv. "I'm going to do everything backwards of backwards from now on."

6

No one knew why Viv did everything backwards. "It might be because we named her Viv," said her father. "Her name is the same if you read it forwards or backwards."

1

Ⓐ

At her birthday party, Viv put the frosting on the cake before she baked it.

"Viv, what have you done?" asked her friends.

"This cake is a mess!"

4

The Front of The Book BY B. Gin Here

She read books back to front.

3

Viv ate dinner for breakfast.

2

Viv gave all her birthday presents back to her friends. Her friends were all very happy when they left, but Viv wasn't. She realized she didn't get any presents!

5

Lost in the Snow

"You took a wrong turn. But I can see you used your heads. I'm very proud of you," said their dad. "And I sure am glad we found you!"

11

Jack and Jessica crawled quickly out of the snow cave.

"Dad!" they shouted as they ran to their father.

They all hugged tightly together.

10

(A)

The twins, Jack and Jessica, loved to ski. They were even better than their dad. In fact, they were way ahead of him on the ski slope.

1

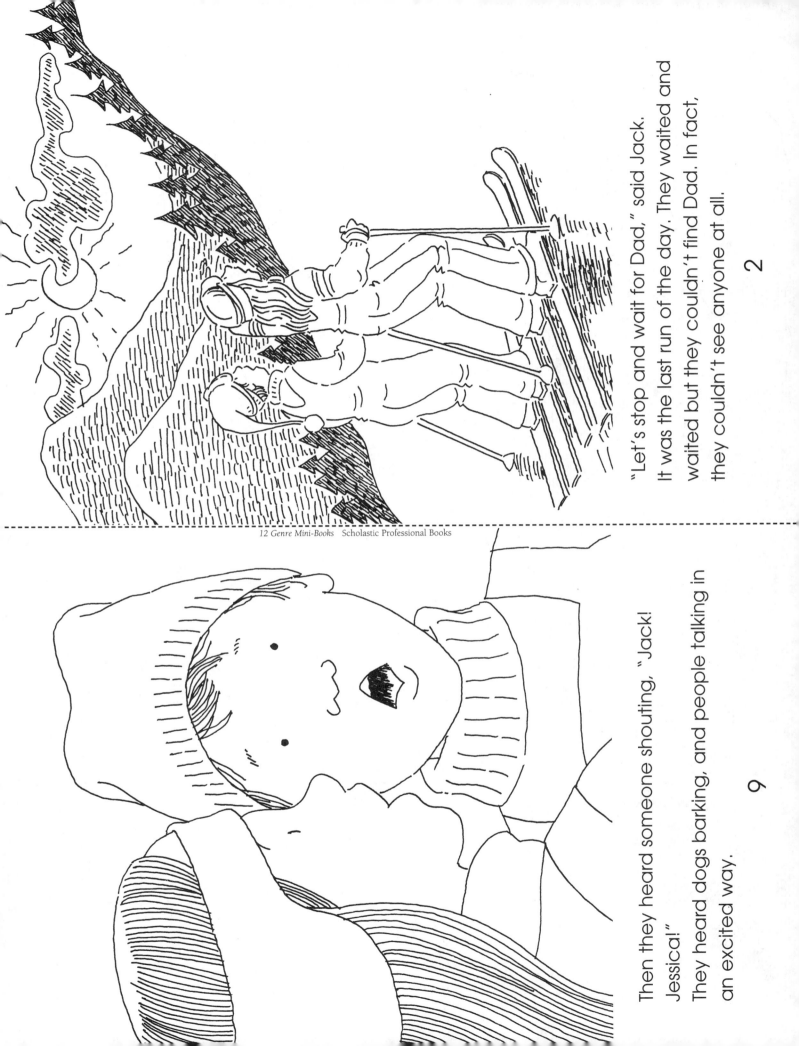

"Let's stop and wait for Dad," said Jack. It was the last run of the day. They waited and waited but they couldn't find Dad. In fact, they couldn't see anyone at all.

2

Then they heard someone shouting, "Jack! Jessica!" They heard dogs barking, and people talking in an excited way.

9

Jack and Jessica huddled together for over an hour to keep their hands and feet warm. It was getting colder.

8

Ⓑ

"We must have taken a wrong turn off the path," said Jessica.
"Hello, hello, does anyone hear us?" they yelled.
But no one yelled back.

3

The sun was going down. The twins became worried about spending the night on the cold mountain.

"Let's build a snow cave," said Jack. "I saw that on TV."

4

Inside the cave, Jack and Jessica searched their pockets. They found granola bars they had packed for a snack.

"We'll have to eat this food a little at a time," said Jack.

7

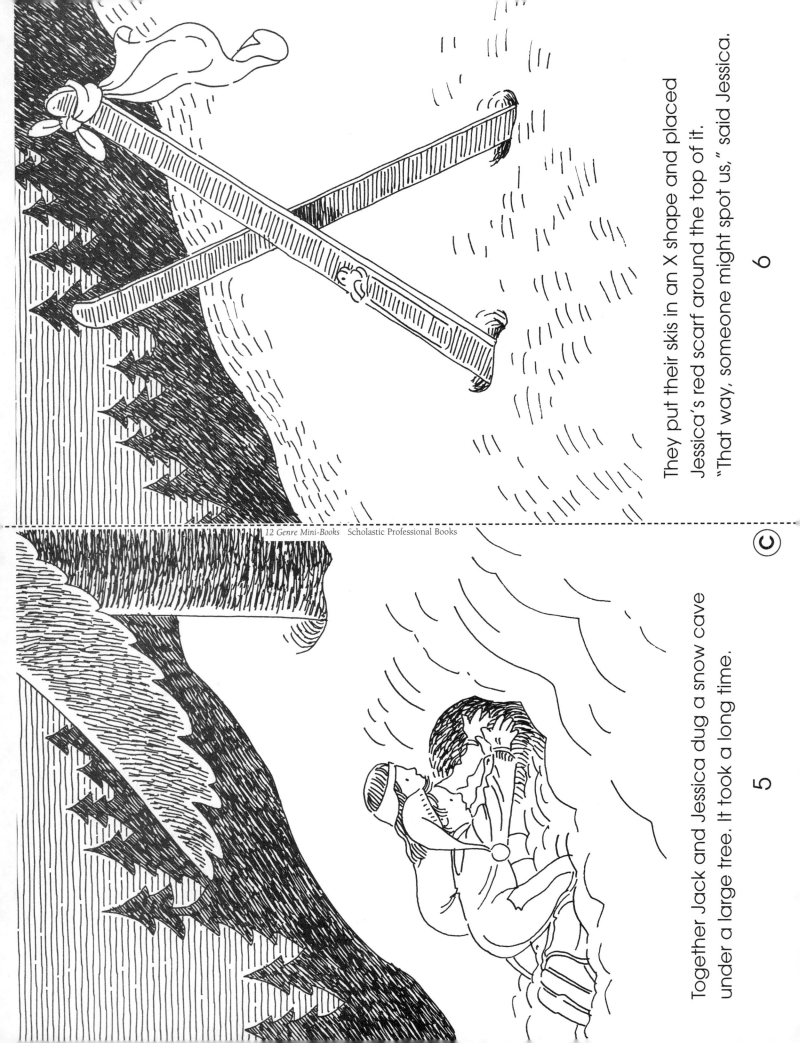

They put their skis in an X shape and placed Jessica's red scarf around the top of it. "That way, someone might spot us," said Jessica.

6

Ⓒ

Together Jack and Jessica dug a snow cave under a large tree. It took a long time.

5

The Mystery of the Missing Cat Food

Joe and I gave each other a thumbs up. We had solved the mystery of the missing cat food!

11

In came Rap, wagging his tail.
"He's been getting a bit chubby lately, hasn't he?" said Mr. Green.

10

It all started the morning that Snowflake's cat food was missing from her bowl.

Ⓐ

1

"It must be a mouse," my brother Joe said.

"But a little mouse just couldn't eat that much food," I said.

"It must be something bigger."

2

Next, we went to see Rap's owner.

"At night, I just let Rap out for a short run in the dark. He always comes right back," said Mr. Green.

9

First we went to see Mrs. Brown, the lady down the street. She owned Shadow.

"We never let Shadow out without a leash," she said. "It couldn't be Shadow."

8

Ⓑ

"Let's put out flour all over the kitchen floor. That way we can get some footprints to study," I said.

3

When we woke up, we had our prints—lots of them.

4

Joe and I made a list of the dogs in the neighborhood. The only small dogs we knew were Shadow and Rap.

7

Next, we had to figure out how big a dog.
"That dog is getting through the cat door so it
must be as small as a cat," said Joe.

6

Ⓒ

With a book on animal prints from the library,
we narrowed it down to a dog.

5

The Big Race

Lisa was disappointed she hadn't won "the big race" that year. But she told herself she could win next year. Looking back, she wasn't at all sorry she'd stopped to help her friend.

11

Lisa and Kevin didn't win anything. In fact, Kevin had tripped on a rock and had twisted his ankle.

10

Ⓐ

The Big Race
Today at 10am!

Every May, Lisa's school had "The Big Race." All the fastest runners would run around the school building to decide who was the fastest of all.

1

This year Lisa felt like she had a good chance to win. The only one who could beat her was her best friend, Kevin. Lisa and Kevin had been running every week with Lisa's sister, who was a star on the high school track team.

2

Jane Taylor whizzed past both of them and won the race.

9

She kneeled down and asked Kevin what was wrong. Some teachers came running over, too.

8

Ⓑ

The day of the race Mrs. Dean, the principal, told everyone to line up. "On your mark, get set, go!" she yelled.

3

Lisa got a good start and so did Kevin. They ran together, side by side, around the first corner and around the second corner.

4

Lisa couldn't say what made her do it, but she turned around and jogged back to the spot where Kevin had fallen.

7

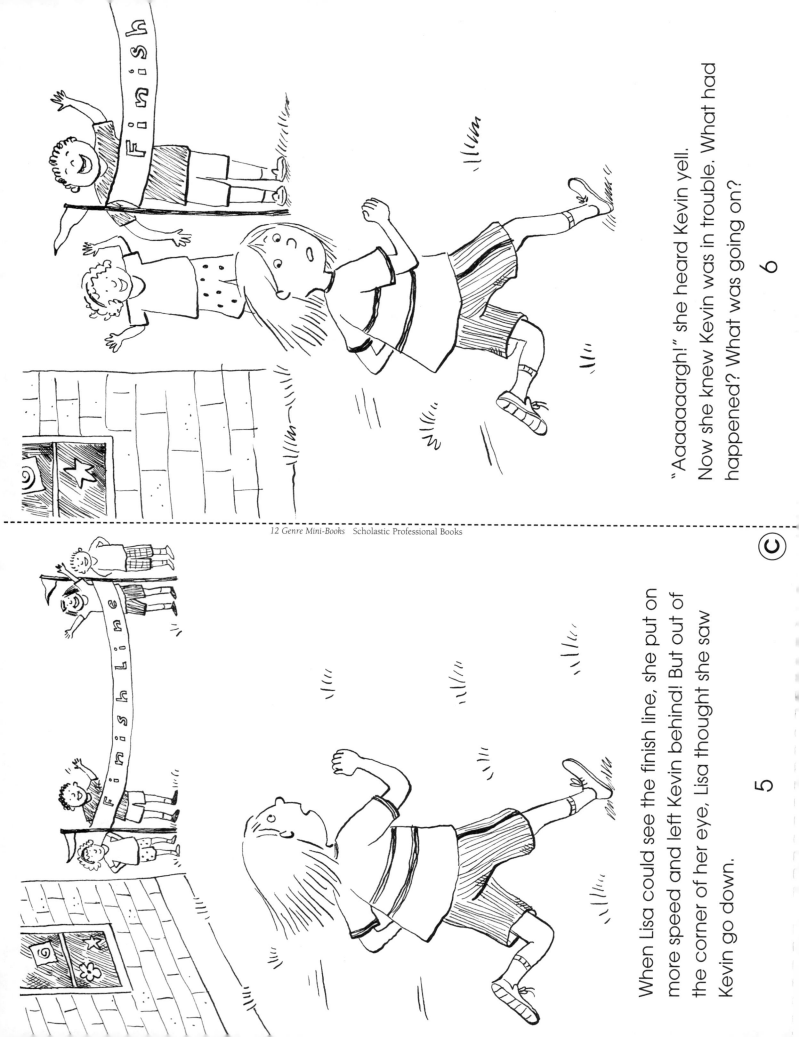

"Aaaaaargh!" she heard Kevin yell. Now she knew Kevin was in trouble. What had happened? What was going on?

6

Ⓒ

When Lisa could see the finish line, she put on more speed and left Kevin behind! But out of the corner of her eye, Lisa thought she saw Kevin go down.

5

Space Scooters on Mars

Kate and Ben each kept a red rock in their bedrooms to remind them of their trip. They both looked forward to seeing their friends on Mars again.

"Only two years to go!" laughed Ben.

11

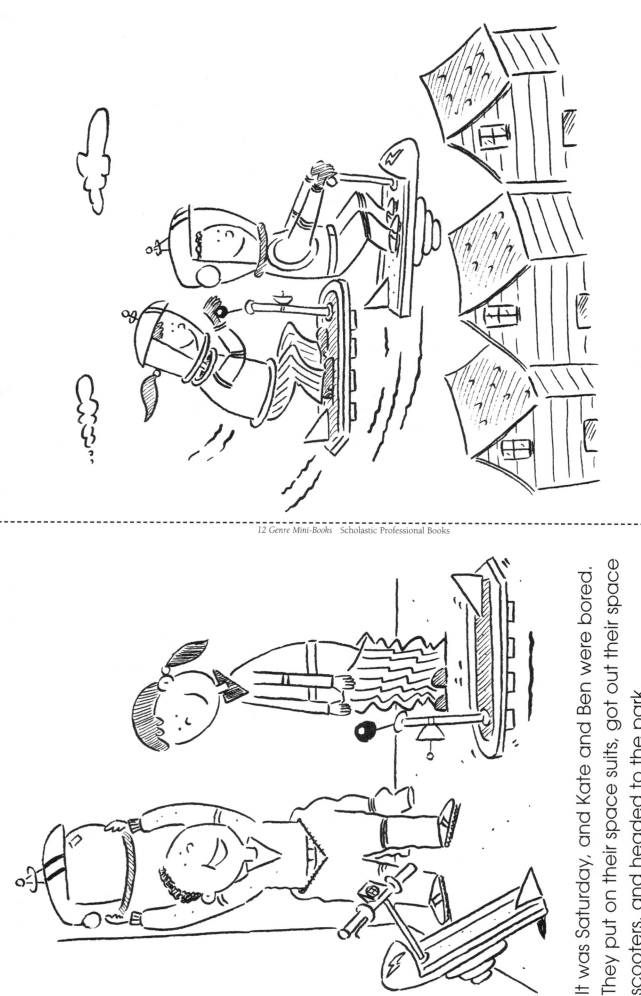

Back in Earth's gravity, Kate and Ben felt a little wobbly. But they climbed on their space scooters and whizzed home.

10

(A)

It was Saturday, and Kate and Ben were bored. They put on their space suits, got out their space scooters, and headed to the park.

"Let's go to Mars," said Kate. "The Earth and Mars are lined up just right for a trip today. It happens only about once every two years!"

1

"You know, the aliens on Mars aren't always friendly," said Ben.

"Come on, let's try it anyway," said Kate. "We'll bring plenty of water. That's one thing Mars doesn't have."

2

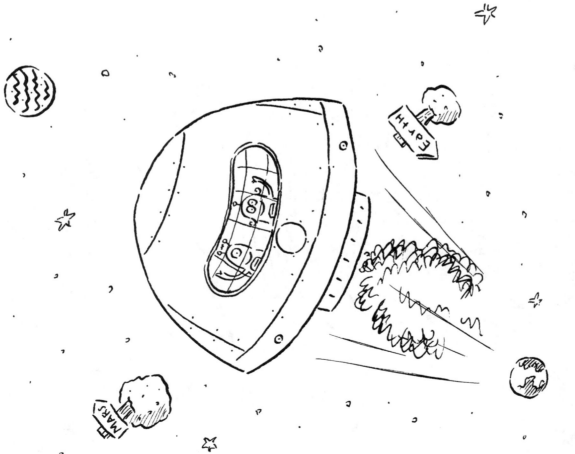

"See you when the planets line up again," said Kate.

"They don't understand us...or do they?" said Ben as they watched the spaceship lift off.

9

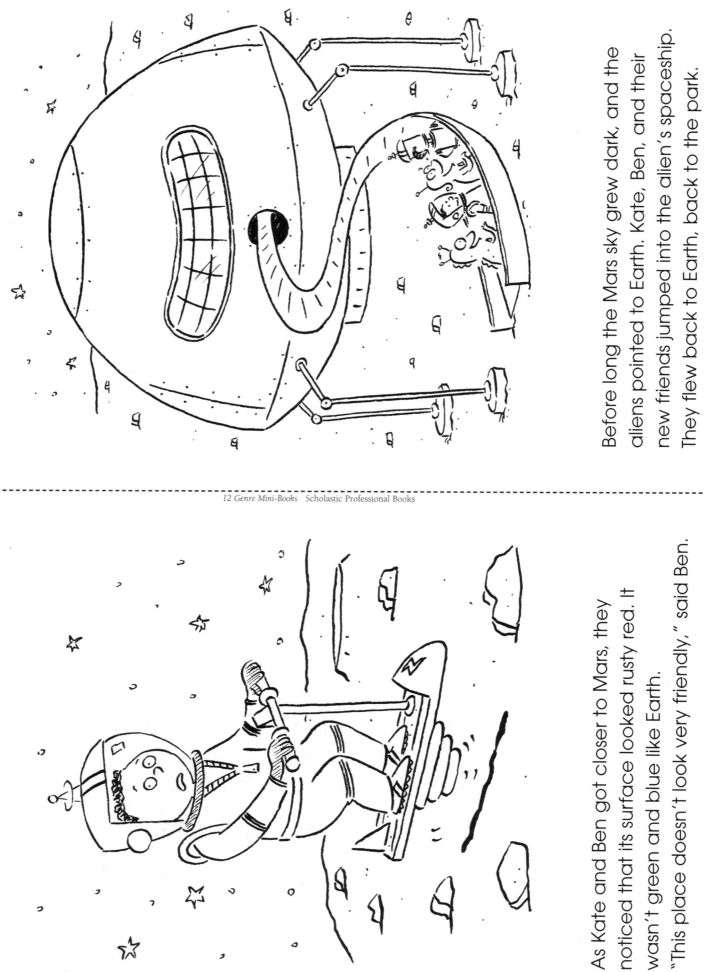

Before long the Mars sky grew dark, and the aliens pointed to Earth. Kate, Ben, and their new friends jumped into the alien's spaceship. They flew back to Earth, back to the park.

8

Ⓑ

As Kate and Ben got closer to Mars, they noticed that its surface looked rusty red. It wasn't green and blue like Earth.
"This place doesn't look very friendly," said Ben.

3

Kate and Ben landed with a bump on the rocks. When they stepped onto Mars, all they could see were rocks, sand, and dust. Suddenly, they heard voices.

"Someone's coming. We'd better hide," said Kate.

4

The aliens pointed to their own space bikes. So Kate and Ben rode those bikes around and around. Soon, they were covered in red dust.

7

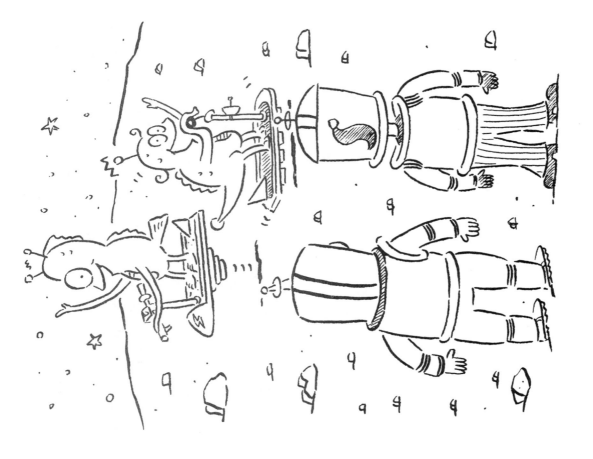

"Those aliens act like they're our age," said Ben. "Let's go out and meet them." Kate and Ben climbed out of the hole and the aliens waved hello.

6

Ⓒ

From their hiding place inside a crater hole, they could see two aliens walking. At first, the aliens looked strange and scary. But when the aliens stopped to look at Kate and Ben's scooters, they smiled. A moment later they hopped on the scooters and rode around in circles.

5

Tom Thumb

The King was so delighted, he gave Tom and his family all the gold they needed. He also had a tiny suit of armor made for his little friend. Tom Thumb lived happily ever after at the castle, riding a mouse and waving a needle for his sword.

7

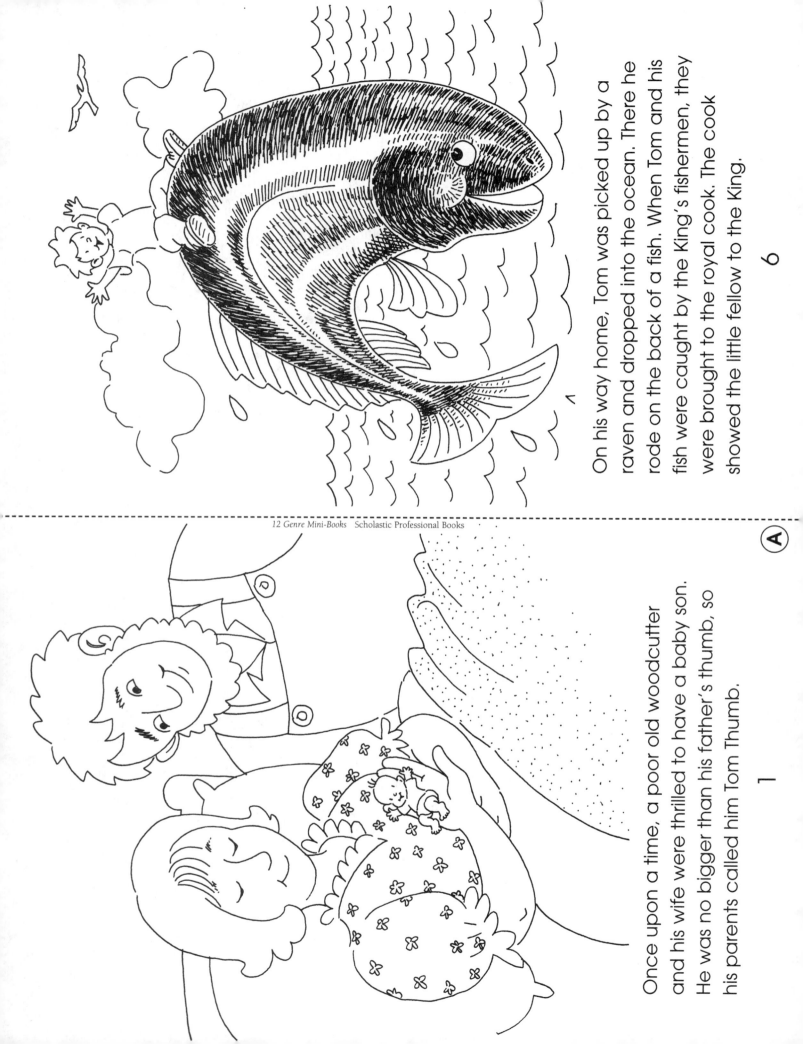

On his way home, Tom was picked up by a raven and dropped into the ocean. There he rode on the back of a fish. When Tom and his fish were caught by the King's fishermen, they were brought to the royal cook. The cook showed the little fellow to the King.

6

Once upon a time, a poor old woodcutter and his wife were thrilled to have a baby son. He was no bigger than his father's thumb, so his parents called him Tom Thumb.

1

Ⓐ

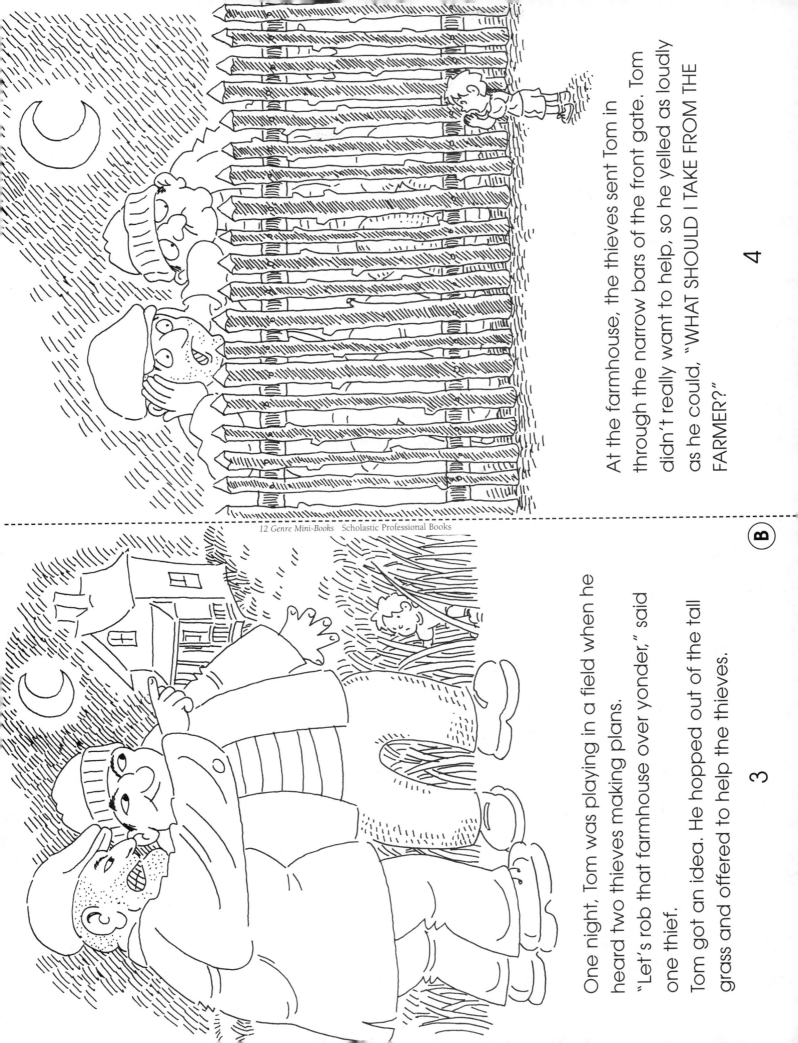

At the farmhouse, the thieves sent Tom in through the narrow bars of the front gate. Tom didn't really want to help, so he yelled as loudly as he could, "WHAT SHOULD I TAKE FROM THE FARMER?"

4

One night, Tom was playing in a field when he heard two thieves making plans.

"Let's rob that farmhouse over yonder," said one thief.

Tom got an idea. He hopped out of the tall grass and offered to help the thieves.

3

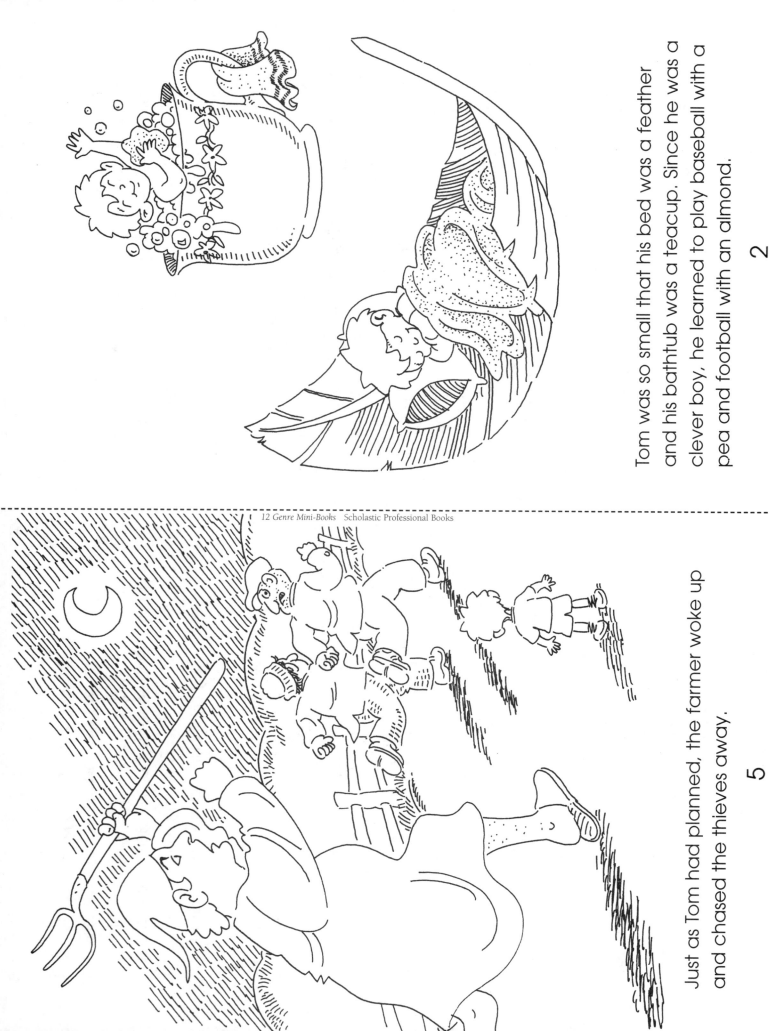

Tom was so small that his bed was a feather and his bathtub was a teacup. Since he was a clever boy, he learned to play baseball with a pea and football with an almond.

2

Just as Tom had planned, the farmer woke up and chased the thieves away.

5

Paul Bunyan and Babe the Blue Ox

Once their logging work was done, Paul and Babe found a place to live in the woods of Maine. When they weren't fishing and hunting, Paul and Babe loved to plant trees and watch them grow.

11

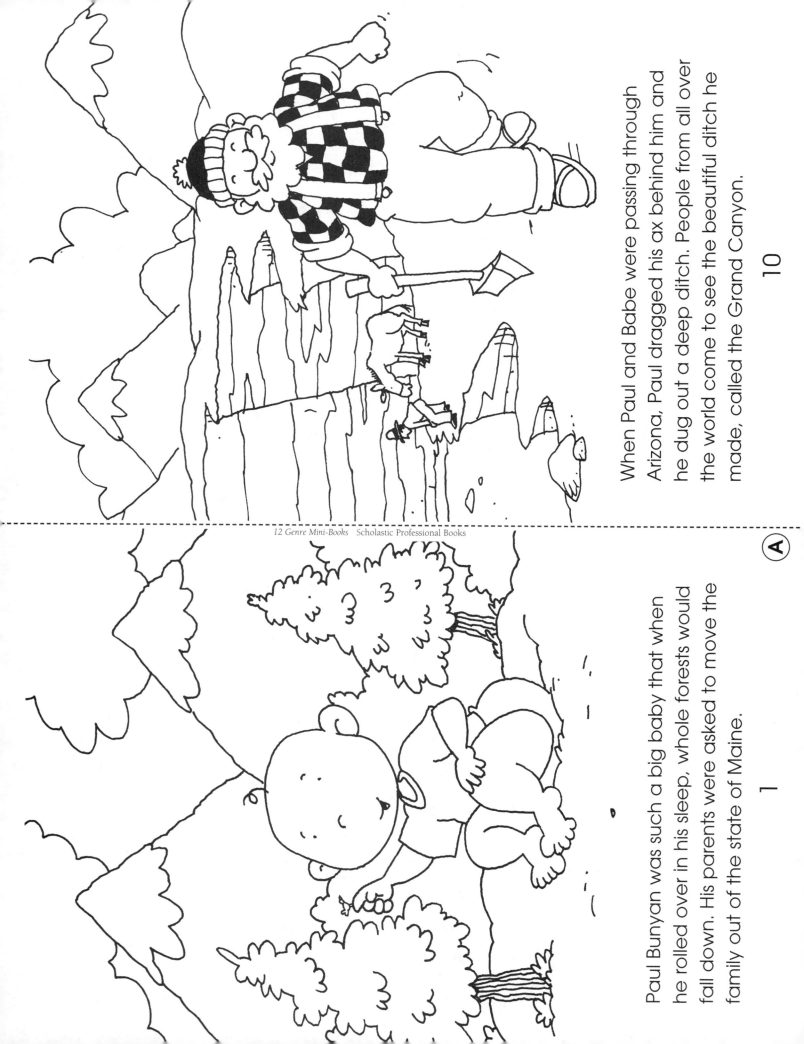

When Paul and Babe were passing through Arizona, Paul dragged his ax behind him and he dug out a deep ditch. People from all over the world come to see the beautiful ditch he made, called the Grand Canyon.

10

Paul Bunyan was such a big baby that when he rolled over in his sleep, whole forests would fall down. His parents were asked to move the family out of the state of Maine.

1

A

So it's no surprise that once Paul found Babe the Blue Ox, they were always together. You see, Babe was the biggest ox you ever saw. The distance between his eyes was said to be 42 ax handles long.

2

One step was as long as a mile for both Paul and Babe. So it didn't take them long to make their way across the United States.

9

With Babe's help, Paul and his men chopped down almost all the trees in Iowa, South Dakota, and North Dakota. The farmers there have been planting on that flat land ever since.

8

B

As a grown man, Paul became a logger. He cut down trees all across the United States, when it was a new country.

3

Paul and Babe made a great team. Babe was so large she could pull a whole forest of trees behind her. People used the wood to build homes and barns.

4

Of course, Paul put seven gallons of maple syrup on his pancakes! What an eating team they made!

7

To feed Babe was a big job, too. He ate about four tons of grain at one meal and nearly the same amount of hay.

6

©

When Babe was thirsty, Paul dug out five large lakes so the ox would have plenty to drink. Those lakes are famous now. They're known as the Great Lakes.

5

Name _____

All About Spiders
Nonfiction

1. Nonfiction gives a reader lots of facts (true information). What facts in *All About Spiders* did you

already know? _____

_____

_____

2. When writing a nonfiction book, authors often do research. Where would you look for facts and

information about spiders? _____

_____

_____

3. What topics about spiders were not covered in this book? (Example: exact sizes of spiders.)

List two. _____

_____

_____

4. What other information would you like to know about spiders? Write two questions you would

like answers to. _____

_____

_____

5. Complete the Genre Web. Write "Nonfiction" in the center rectangle.

6. What makes *All About Spiders* nonfiction? _____

_____

_____

✦ ✦ ✦ ✏ Writing Prompt ✦ ✦ ✦

Now it's your turn to write nonfiction. Think about a subject that you know a lot about
and fill in the Story Map to organize your thoughts. Then start writing! Some ideas:

 ✳ an animal or bug
 ✳ an activity such as riding a scooter or playing soccer
 ✳ a season of the year

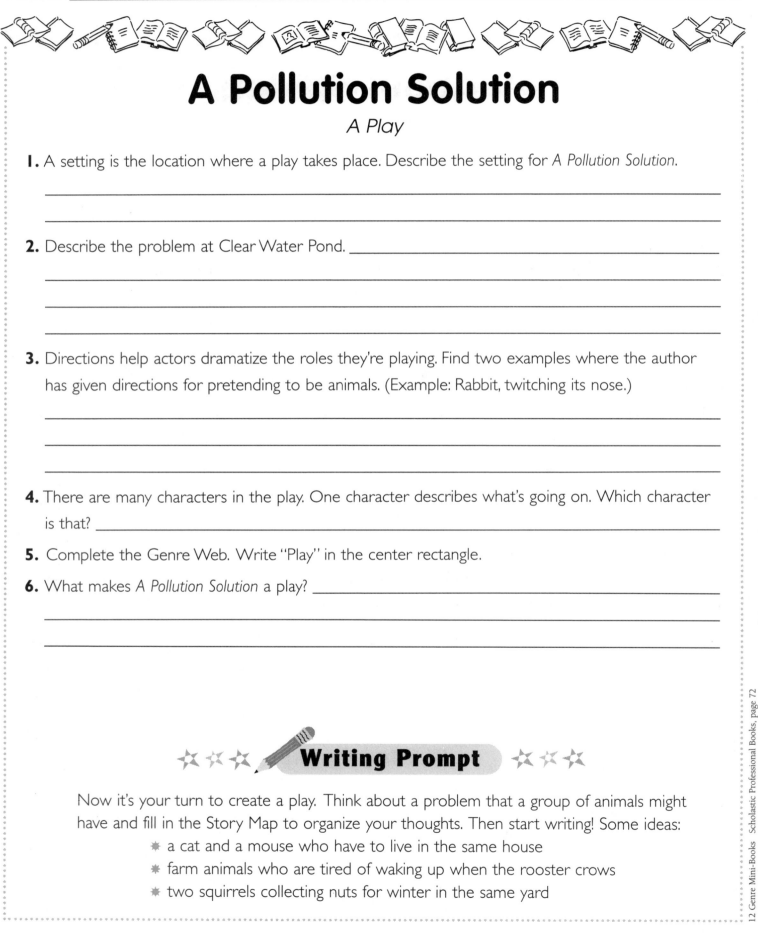

A Pollution Solution
A Play

1. A setting is the location where a play takes place. Describe the setting for *A Pollution Solution*.

_____

_____

2. Describe the problem at Clear Water Pond. _____

_____

_____

_____

3. Directions help actors dramatize the roles they're playing. Find two examples where the author has given directions for pretending to be animals. (Example: Rabbit, twitching its nose.)

_____

_____

_____

4. There are many characters in the play. One character describes what's going on. Which character is that? _____

5. Complete the Genre Web. Write "Play" in the center rectangle.

6. What makes *A Pollution Solution* a play? _____

_____

_____

★ ★ ★ ✏ **Writing Prompt** ★ ★ ★

Now it's your turn to create a play. Think about a problem that a group of animals might have and fill in the Story Map to organize your thoughts. Then start writing! Some ideas:
- ✳ a cat and a mouse who have to live in the same house
- ✳ farm animals who are tired of waking up when the rooster crows
- ✳ two squirrels collecting nuts for winter in the same yard

Name _____

Jane Goodall and the Chimps
Biography

1. Why do you think the author chose to write about Jane Goodall? _____
_____
_____

2. Reread the part about Jane Goodall's childhood. What hints did you have from the author that Jane might become an animal scientist? _____
_____
_____
_____

3. Why do people invite Jane Goodall to share what she knows about chimps? What can we learn from her? _____
_____
_____

4. When writing a biography, authors often do research. How would you find information about Jane Goodall? _____
_____
_____

5. Complete the Genre Web. Write "Biography" in the center rectangle.

6. What makes *Jane Goodall and the Chimps* a biography? _____
_____
_____

✦✦✦ Writing Prompt ✦✦✦

Now it's your turn to write a biography. Think about a famous person or someone in your family and fill in the Story Map to organize your thoughts. Then start writing! Some ideas:
* something special she did
* some way he helped people
* an unusual job or adventure she had

Escape in the Night
Historical Fiction

1. Historical fiction is a made-up story that takes place in a real time in the past. What part of this
story is fiction (made up)? _____
_____

2. What real information from history has the author shared in this story? (Example: Ohio was a free
state.) List three. _____
_____
_____
_____

3. What is the main problem the characters in this story face? _____
_____
_____
_____

4. How did Tina's father feel when the family arrived in Ohio? What clues does the author give us?
_____
_____
_____

5. Complete the Genre Web. Write "Historical Fiction" in the center rectangle.

6. What makes *Escape in the Night* historical fiction? _____
_____
_____

✮✮✮ ✏ Writing Prompt ✮✮✮

Now it's your turn to write historical fiction. Think about a story that could take place in
the past and fill in the Story Map to organize your thoughts. Then start writing! Some ideas:
* a child who is at the first Thanksgiving with the Pilgrims and Indians
* children who must help their father build a log cabin before winter comes
* a boy who hides on Christopher Columbus's ship

Name _____

All Sorts of Animal Poems
Poetry

1. Sometimes the words in poems have the same beginning sound. This is called *alliteration*. List two words from "The Catfight" with same beginning sound. _____

_____

2. When words sound like what they mean, it's called *onomatopoeia*. Find some words in the poem "The Catfight" that sound like what they mean. (Example: yowwwling) _____

_____

_____

3. Poems often make the reader feel feelings. Reread "My Dog is Missing." Do you feel the same at the end of the poem as you felt when reading its beginning? Why or why not? _____

_____

_____

_____

4. Some poems rhyme and some don't. What are some of the rhyming words in "Being an Elephant"?

ease and _____

eat and _____

5. Poets sometimes make up new words for their poems. Find six funny new words from the poem "Rhinocerecess." _____

_____

_____

6. Complete the Genre Web. Write "Poetry" in the center rectangle.

⋆ ⋆ ⋆ ✏ **Writing Prompt** ⋆ ⋆ ⋆

Now it's your turn to write a poem. Think about an animal and fill in the Story Map to organize your thoughts. Then start writing! Will it rhyme or not? Some ideas:

   ❋ a puppy who wishes she were a bird
   ❋ a kitten who's just getting to know her new family
   ❋ an fish who likes to be alone

Name _____

Backwards Viv

Humorous Fiction

1. In a humorous story, the main character usually has a funny habit or trait. What's funny about Viv?

_____

_____

2. Usually the character does silly things. What was your favorite silly thing Viv did? Explain.

_____

_____

_____

3. What other activities do you imagine Viv does backwards? List two. _____

_____

_____

4. In humorous stories, the way the character gets out of a big mess is often a surprise. How does Viv change her "backwards" life? _____

_____

_____

_____

5. Complete the Genre Web. Write "Humorous Story" in the center rectangle.

6. What makes *Backwards Viv* humorous? _____

_____

_____

✬ ✬ ✬ ✐ **Writing Prompt** ✬ ✬ ✬

Now it's your turn to write a humorous story. Think about a funny problem that a person might have and fill in the Story Map to organize your thoughts. Then start writing! Some ideas:

   ✳ a child that has way too many dogs, cats, or goldfish
   ✳ a child who eats only one kind of food
   ✳ a bird who thinks she is a dog

Lost in the Snow

Adventure

1. An adventure story usually has a big problem that is exciting or dangerous. What is the problem in *Lost in the Snow?* _____

_____

2. Many adventure stories are about surviving in a dangerous situation. What do the characters in this story do to survive? Write each step in the boxes below:

1st	2nd	3rd	4th

3. Many adventure stories are about girls and boys just like you. How are the characters in this story like you (or like people you know)? Explain. _____

_____

_____

4. Complete the Genre Web. Write "Adventure" in the center rectangle.

5. What makes *Lost in the Snow* an adventure story? _____

_____

_____

★ ★ ★ **Writing Prompt** ★ ★ ★

Now it's your turn to write an adventure story. Think about an exciting problem
and fill in the Story Map to organize your thoughts. Then start writing! Some ideas:

   ✳ a child gets lost in a giant Thanksgiving Day parade
   ✳ a family canoeing down a river runs into a storm
   ✳ a family hiking in the woods takes a wrong turn

Name _____

The Mystery of the Missing Cat Food
Mystery

1. A mystery has a puzzling problem to be solved. What is the puzzle in this mystery? _____

_____

_____

2. Mysteries have clues that help the reader and the story characters solve the mystery. What are
some of the clues the author has given you? _____

_____

_____

_____

3. Most mysteries seem like they could really happen. Explain why you think this mystery could really
happen. _____

_____

_____

_____

4. Mysteries usually have a character or characters that solve the mystery. Who solves the mystery in
this story? _____

_____

5. Complete the Genre Web. Write "Mystery" in the center rectangle.

6. What makes *The Mystery of the Missing Cat Food* a mystery? _____

_____

_____

☆☆☆ ✏ Writing Prompt ☆☆☆

Now it's your turn to write a mystery. Think about a puzzling problem and fill in
the Story Map to organize your thoughts. Then start writing! Some ideas:
* The Mystery of the Missing Homework
* The Mystery of the Missing Teddy Bear
* The Mystery of the Missing Soccer Ball

The Big Race
Realistic Fiction

1. Realistic fiction means the story is made up but it could happen. Modern means it takes place now. In realistic fiction, a main character often has an important decision to make. What decision did Lisa have to make? _____

_____

_____

_____

2. Sometimes stories teach a lesson. What lesson could you learn from this story? _____

_____

_____

3. How did Lisa end up looking like a winner even though she didn't win? _____

_____

_____

4. What would you have done if you were Lisa? Explain. _____

_____

_____

_____

5. Complete the Genre Web. Write " Realistic Fiction" in the center rectangle.

6. What makes *The Big Race* realistic? _____

_____

_____

✭ ✭ ✭ ✎ Writing Prompt ✭ ✭ ✭

Now it's your turn to write realistic fiction. Think about a problem that two people might have and fill in the Story Map to organize your thoughts. Then start writing! Some ideas:

* brothers who are saving up for the same bike at the sports store
* friends who try out for the same part in a play
* friends who want the same position on the baseball team

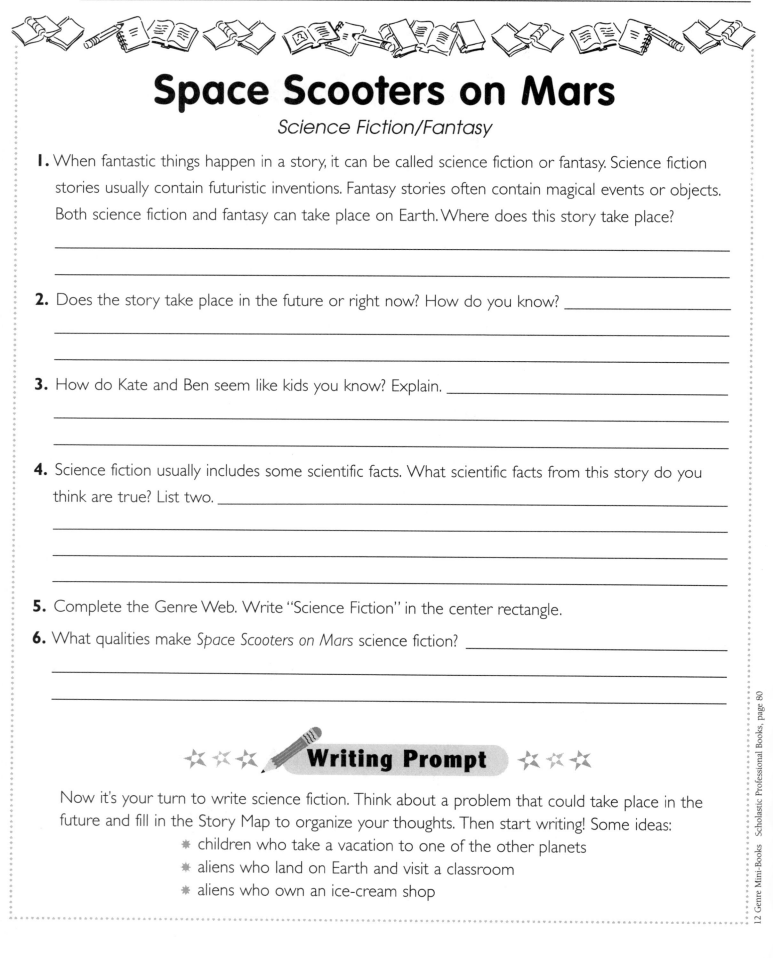

Space Scooters on Mars

Science Fiction/Fantasy

1. When fantastic things happen in a story, it can be called science fiction or fantasy. Science fiction stories usually contain futuristic inventions. Fantasy stories often contain magical events or objects. Both science fiction and fantasy can take place on Earth. Where does this story take place?

_____

_____

2. Does the story take place in the future or right now? How do you know? _____

_____

_____

3. How do Kate and Ben seem like kids you know? Explain. _____

_____

_____

4. Science fiction usually includes some scientific facts. What scientific facts from this story do you think are true? List two. _____

_____

_____

_____

5. Complete the Genre Web. Write "Science Fiction" in the center rectangle.

6. What qualities make *Space Scooters on Mars* science fiction? _____

_____

_____

✦✦✦ ✏️ **Writing Prompt** ✦✦✦

Now it's your turn to write science fiction. Think about a problem that could take place in the future and fill in the Story Map to organize your thoughts. Then start writing! Some ideas:
* children who take a vacation to one of the other planets
* aliens who land on Earth and visit a classroom
* aliens who own an ice-cream shop

Name _____

Tom Thumb
Fairy Tale

1. Fairy tales are favorite stories that have been told over and over again. Why do you think Tom Thumb is retold to children year after year? _____
_____
_____

2. Fairy tales often begin with the words "Once upon a time." What other stories can you think of that begin that way? _____
_____
_____

3. Did Tom help the farmer or the thieves? Explain. _____
_____
_____
_____

4. Tom had many adventures in this story. Which one is your favorite and why? _____
_____
_____
_____

5. Complete the Genre Web. Write "Fairy Tale" in the center rectangle.

6. What makes *Tom Thumb* a fairy tale? _____
_____
_____

✠ ✠ ✠ ✏ **Writing Prompt** ✠ ✠ ✠

Now it's your turn to write your own version of a favorite fairy tale. Think about a fairy tale you know well and fill in the Story Map to organize your thoughts. Then start writing! Some ideas:
 ✳ The Three Little Pigs
 ✳ Jack and the Beanstalk
 ✳ Little Red Riding Hood

Name _____

Paul Bunyan and Babe the Blue Ox

Tall Tale

1. Tall tales often take place in the past. What clues did the author give us that this story took place in the past? _____

_____

_____

2. There is a lot of exaggeration in a tall tale. What can Paul Bunyan do that real people cannot do?

_____

_____

3. The story in a tall tale could never happen. But there are usually some true facts or real places in it. What places in this tall tale are real? _____

_____

_____

_____

4. Tall tales are usually funny. Name one funny thing that happened in this story. _____

_____

_____

5. Complete the Genre Web. Write "Tall Tale" in the center rectangle.

6. What makes *Paul Bunyan and Babe the Blue Ox* a tall tale? _____

_____

_____

⋆ ⋆ ⋆ **Writing Prompt** ⋆ ⋆ ⋆

Now it's your turn to write a tall tale. Think about a character who is exaggerated in some way and fill in the Story Map to organize your thoughts. Then start writing! Be sure to tell some of the interesting adventures the character has. Some ideas:

  ✳ a person who lives in the woods and makes friends with bears and wolves
  ✳ a person who walks across the whole United States cleaning up the air, water, and land
  ✳ a person who swims across oceans and rides on the backs of whales

Name _____

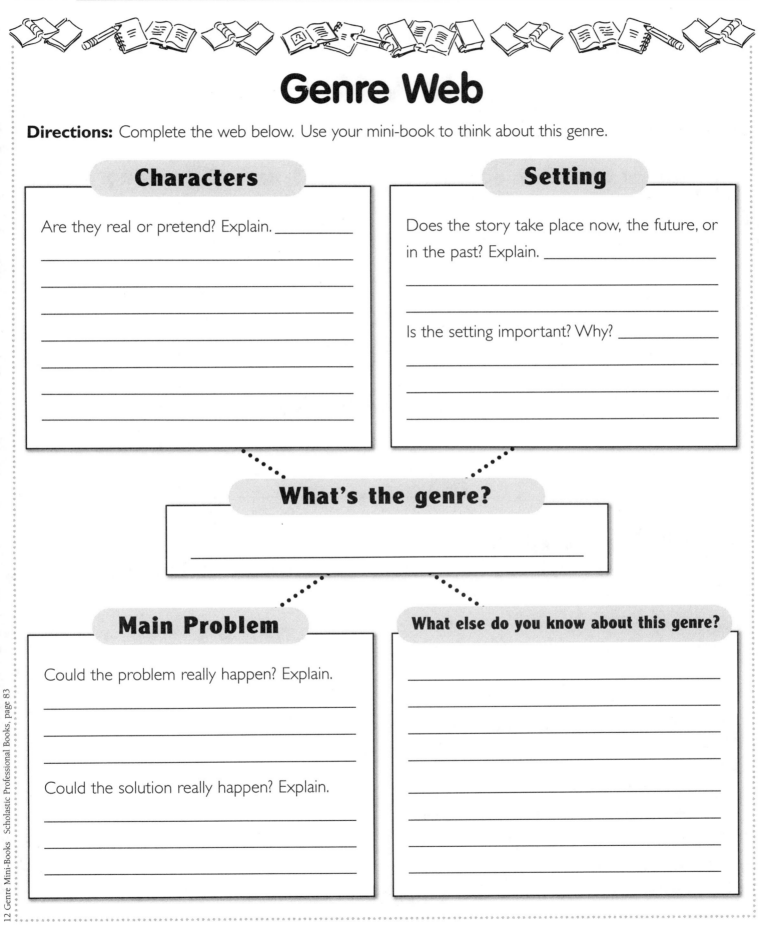

Genre Web

Directions: Complete the web below. Use your mini-book to think about this genre.

Characters

Are they real or pretend? Explain. _____
_____
_____
_____
_____
_____
_____

Setting

Does the story take place now, the future, or
in the past? Explain. _____
_____
_____

Is the setting important? Why? _____
_____
_____
_____

What's the genre?

_____

Main Problem

Could the problem really happen? Explain.
_____
_____
_____

Could the solution really happen? Explain.
_____
_____
_____

What else do you know about this genre?

_____
_____
_____
_____
_____
_____
_____
_____

Name _____

Story Map

Directions: Fill in this story map to organize your ideas before you begin writing.

Who or what is it about?

Characters: _____

_____

_____

_____

Topic: _____

What's the setting?

Time: _____

Place: _____

_____

_____

_____

What's the genre?

_____

Story title: _____

What happens in the story?

Beginning: _____

Middle: _____

End: _____

How else will your writing fit the genre?

_____

_____

_____

_____

_____

_____

_____

_____

Is there a main problem?

Explain: _____

_____

How is it solved: _____

_____

Booklinks

Nonfiction
The Icky Bug Book by Jerry Pallotta (Charlesbridge, 1990)
Extremely Weird Frogs by Sarah Lovett (Econo-Clad Books, 1999)
To Space and Back by Sally Ride with Susan Okie (Lothrop, Lee & Shepard, 1992)
The Story of the White House by Kate Waters (Scholastic, 1992)
Stars by Jennifer Dussling (Grosset & Dunlap, 1996)
What Makes a Magnet? by Franklyn M. Branley (HarperCollins, 1996)

Plays
The Big Book of Thematic Plays compiled and edited by Tracey West (Scholastic, 2000)
Small Plays for Special Days by Sue Alexander (Clarion Books, 1977)
Giants and Other Plays for Kids by Syd Hoff (G.P. Putnam's Sons, 1973)

Biography
Martin Luther King, Jr.: Free at Last by David A. Adler (Holiday House, 1998)
The Life and Work of...Leonardo da Vinci by Sean Connolly (Heineman First Library, 2000)
J.K. Rowling: The Wizard Behind Harry Potter by Marc Shapiro (Griffin, 2000)
A Young Painter: The Life and Paintings of Wang Yani—China's Extraordinary Young Artist
   by Zheng Ahensun and Alice Low (Scholastic, 1989)
Walking the Road to Freedom: A Story of Sojourner Truth by Jeri Ferris (Carolrhoda Books, 1989)
Amelia Earhart: Adventure in the Sky by Francene Sabin (Troll Communications, 1989)
Deborah Sampson Goes to War by Bryne Stevens (Carolrhoda Books, 1984)

Historical Fiction
Molly's Pilgrim by Barbara Cohen (Beech Tree Books, 1998)
The Josefina Story Quilt by Eleanor Coerr (HarperTrophy, 1986)
Wagon Wheels by Barbara Brenner (Econo-Clad Books, 1999)
Dust for Dinner by Ann Turner (HarperCollins, 1995)
Kate Shelley and the Midnight Express by Margaret K. Wetterer (Carolrhoda Books, 1990)
Daniel's Duck by Clyde Robert Bulla (Harper & Row, 1979)
Chang's Paper Pony by Eleanor Coerr (HarperCollins, 1988)
Stradivari's Singing Violin by Catherine Deverell (Carolrhoda Books, 1992)
An American Army of Two by Janet Greeson (Carolrhoda Books, 1992)

Poetry
Sunflakes: Poems for Children selected by Lilian Moore (Clarion Books, 1992)
The Random House Book of Poetry for Children selected by Jack Prelutsky (Random House, 1983)
Rainy Rainy Saturday by Jack Prelutsky (Greenwillow Books, 1980)
I Like Stars by Margaret Wise Brown (A Golden Book, 1982)
Surprises by Lee Bennett Hopkins (Harper & Row, 1984)
Blast Off! Poems About Space selected by Lee Bennett Hopkins (HarperCollins, 1995)

Humorous Fiction
Amelia Bedelia by Peggy Parish (Scholastic, 1963)
There Is a Carrot in My Ear and Other Noodle Tales retold by Alvin Schwartz (Harper & Row, 1982)
Junie B. Jones and Some Sneaky Peeky Spying by Barbara Park (Random House, 1994)
If You Give a Mouse a Cookie by Laura Numeroff (Harper & Row, 1985)
Ralph's Secret Weapon by Steven Kellogg (E.P. Dutton, 1983)
Ferret in the Bedroom, Lizards in the Fridge by Bill Wallace (Holiday House, 1986)
Morris and Boris, Three Stories by Bernard Wiseman (Dodd, Mead & Co., 1974)
The Gollywhopper Egg by Anne Rockwell (Macmillan, 1974)

Booklinks ☆ ☆ ☆ (Cont.)

Adventure

Afternoon on the Amazon by Mary Pope Osborne (Random House, 1995)
The Big Balloon Race by Eleanor Coerr (Harper & Row, 1981)
Stone Fox by John Reynolds Gardiner (Thomas Y. Crowell, 1980)

Mystery

Cam Jansen and the Triceratops Mystery by David A. Adler (Puffin Books, 1995)
Picnic at Mudsock Meadow by Patricia Polacco (Putnam, 1992)
The Mystery of Chimney Rock by Edward Packard (Grolier, 1988)
Detective Mole by Robert Quackenbush (Lothrop, Lee & Shepard, 1976)
Nate the Great by Marjorie Weinman Sharmat (Coward-McCann, 1972)
Clues in the Woods by Peggy Parish (Macmillan, 1968)
Stage Door to Terror, A Miss Mallard Mystery by Robert Quackenbush (Prentice-Hall, 1985)

Realistic Fiction

Henry and Mudge and the Best Day of All by Cynthia Rylant (Macmillan Books for Young Readers, 1995)
Chicken Sunday by Patricia Polacco (Philomel Books, 1992)
Marvin Redpost: Kidnapped at Birth? by Louis Sachar (Random House, 1992)
Amber Brown Is Not a Crayon by Paula Danzinger (Scholastic, 1995)
Sneakers, Seven Stories About a Cat by Margaret Wise Brown (Addison-Wesley, 1955)
Goliath and the Buried Treasure by Terrance Dicks (Barron's, 1984)
Rip-Roaring Russell by Johanna Hurwitz (William Morrow and Company, 1983)

Science Fiction

Commander Toad in Space by Jane Yolen (The Putnam & Grosset Group, 1980)
The Laziest Robot in Zone One by Lillian Hoban (Harper & Row, 1983)
The Space Ship Returns to the Apple Tree by Louis Slobodkin (Macmillan, 1958)

Fantasy

Where the Wild Things Are by Maurice Sendak (HarperCollins, 1988)
My Father's Dragon by Ruth Stiles Gannett (Random House, 1986)
Charlie and the Chocolate Factory by Roald Dahl (Puffin Books, 1998)
Travels of Doctor Dolittle by Al Perkins (Random House, 1967)
The Wingdingdilly by Bill Peet (Houghton Mifflin Co., 1970)

Fairy Tales

The Korean Cinderella by Shirley Climo (HarperCollins, 1993)
Elves and the Shoemaker by Paul Galdone (Econo-Clad Books, 1999)
Gingerbread Boy by Paul Galdone (Clarion Books, 1979)
The Princess and the Pea by Harriet Ziefert (Viking, 1996)
The Frog Prince retold by Edith H. Tarcov (Scholastic, 1993)
A Story, A Story by Gail E. Haley (Atheneum, 1988)
The Woman with the Eggs by Hans Christian Andersen adapted by Jan Wahl (Crown Publishers, 1974)
Three Billy Goats Gruff retold by Patricia and Fredrick McKissack (Children's Press, 1987)

Tall Tales

The Narrow Escapes of Davy Crockett by Ariane Dewey (Greenwillow Books, 1990)
Pecos Bill Rides a Tornado by Wyatt Blassingame (Garrard, 1973)
McBroom's Ear by Sid Fleischman (W.W. Norton & Co., 1969)
The Tea Squall by Ariane Dewey (Greenwillow Books, 1988)
Febold Feboldson by Ariane Dewey (Greenwillow Books, 1984)
Gib Morgan, Oilman by Ariane Dewey (Greenwillow Books, 1987)

Answer Key ✕ ✕ ✕

All About Spiders: Nonfiction
1. Answers will vary.
2. library books, magazines, the Internet, interviews
3. enemies of spiders, how they make silk, tarantulas
4. Answers will vary.
5. Nonfiction: characters are real people, animals, or events; may include a conflict; locale or setting is a real place; contains factual information; may contain scientific words; facts organized by category.
6. Answers may include: Spiders are real creatures; they live in real places like barns and yards; the facts based in research; author includes scientific words related to spiders.

A Pollution Solution: A Play
1. It's a pond with plants and trees on its banks.
2. Humans are littering the pond's shore with trash and garbage.
3. Answers may include: Beaver holding a claw in front of its teeth; Duck flapping its wings; Beaver chopping down trees with its teeth; Snake swaying his head.
4. a narrator
5. Play: may tell a biographical, nonfiction, or fictional story; characters are played by actors who tell the story through conversation; may include a narrator; story setting is re-created for the stage format; props and costumes may be used to help bring the story to life for the audience.
6. Answers may include: Animals are played by actors who tell the story through conversation; the author has provided prop ideas; and stage directions are given for the actors.

Jane Goodall and the Chimps: Biography
1. Answers may include: the author admires Jane's research; has a fondness for chimpanzees; is interested in preserving wildlife habitats.
2. The author wrote that Jane liked to watch animals, had a favorite toy that was a chimpanzee, and waited patiently for a hen to lay an egg.
3. Jane's knowledge about chimpanzees and how they behave helps us understand humans better. She shares what she knows about chimpanzee's habitats and their preservation.
4. Answers may include: library books, the Internet, and interviews.
5. Biography: is a true story of a real person's life; reflects the place and time in which the person lives; shows how the person affects people in important ways; shares facts learned from research; indicates how the author regards the person.
6. Jane Goodall is a real person; the biography tells about her life as a scientist; her research on chimpanzees teaches people about chimpanzees and humans; the details provided show that the author researched Jane Goodall's life; and the author's voice suggests she respects Jane Goodall's work to protect chimpanzees and their habitats.

Escape in the Night: Historical Fiction
1. The characters are not real people. The conversations that they have are pretend.
2. Slaves did not receive pay for their work. Many were beaten by their owners. The members of the Underground Railroad helped slaves escape to freedom in the Northern states by setting out lanterns, quilts, flags, and candles. They fed and hid slaves, protecting them from discovery. Runaway slaves often used the North Star to guide them toward freedom.
3. The family is trying to escape slavery to find freedom.
4. Tina's father is happy. The author tells us Tina's father kneeled and kissed the ground of the free state of Ohio.
5. Historical fiction: the characters may be real or fictional; the make-believe story takes place during a real time in the past; the problem is realistic for the time period; the characters speak and behave in real-life ways that reflect the time period; the actual history that is included is based on researched, factual information.
6. Tina and her family are make-believe characters who live during a real time in American history; the Underground Railroad was a real organization whose primary goal was to guide runaway slaves to freedom in the North; and the strategies Tina's family used, like following the North Star and hiding in people's homes are based in historical facts.

All Sorts of Animal Poems: Poetry
1. screeches, scratches
2. grrrowling, screeches, shrieks
3. Answers may include: No. First I felt sad, then I felt happy. At first she is sad that the dog is missing. Then it shows up on her doorstep.
4. ease, trees, and knees; eat and neat
5. rhinocerecess, rhinocerace, rhinocerides, rhinoceromp, rhinocerules, rhinocerow, rhinocerithmetic
6. Poetry: uses words to paint a picture in the reader's mind; may tell a whole story or just illustrate an idea; uses words in playful ways through onomatopoeia, alliteration, rhymes, and rhythm; may be formatted in a variety of ways including: concrete, lists, narrative, free verse, ballad, haiku, sonnets, and more.

Backwards Viv: Humorous Fiction
1. She does everything backwards.
2. Answers will vary.
3. Answers will vary.
4. She decides to do everything backwards of backwards.
5. Humor: characters have funny attributes or behave in silly ways; setting may be real or pretend; the main problem may be unrealistic or realistic but is resolved a funny and often surprising way.
6. Viv does everything backwards; she decides to resolve her problem by doing things backwards of backwards.

Answer Key ✰ ✰ ✰ (Cont.)

Lost in the Snow: Adventure
1. The twins get lost while skiing, and it's getting dark on the mountain.
2. Build a cave, put skis out with red scarf, ration food, huddle together to stay warm
3. Answers will vary.
4. Adventure: the characters are realistic people; the setting is a realistic place; the problem is exciting, often about surviving; the solution is realistic considering the circumstances the characters are in.
5. Jack and Jessica are skiing as children often like to do; they become separated from their father which happens sometimes; use survival strategies to stay safe.

The Mystery of the Missing Cat Food: Mystery
1. Snowflake's cat food is being stolen.
2. The dog was small enough to get in the cat door, the footprints were a dog's, and Rap was gaining weight.
3. Answers will vary.
4. the narrator and her brother Joe
5. Mystery: the fictional story contains an unusual problem or puzzle to solve; the author provides the characters and reader with clues to solve the mystery; the events seem real rather than fantastical; and the main character(s) from the story solve the mystery.
6. Finding the culprit is a puzzling problem to solve; the footprints and Rap's weight gain are clues; and the narrator and her brother Joe solve the mystery.

The Big Race: Realistic Fiction
1. Lisa had to decide whether to help her friend Kevin or win the race.
2. Answers may include: Friendship is more important than winning a race; sometimes it is difficult to be a good friend.
3. She was a good friend to Kevin.
4. Answers will vary.
5. Realistic Fiction: stories contain fictional characters who behave like real people; the setting is in a familiar place during modern times; the problem is common and requires the characters to make a tough decision; the resolution is realistic and addresses the problem in ways that make sense; the conversation fits modern times.
6. Kevin and Lisa behave like real children: lots of schools have races; when Kevin falls, Lisa makes the hard decision to help him.

Space Scooters on Mars: Science Fiction/Fantasy
1. The characters ride scooters from Earth to the surface of Mars.
2. The story must take place in the future since we don't have space scooters now.
3. Answers will vary.
4. Earth and Mars do line up well about once every two years. Mars is reddish and is covered in rocks, sand, and dust. There is no liquid water on Mars. Going from outer space back to Earth does make astronauts dizzy.

5. Science Fiction: a fictional story that takes place in the future; setting is Earth in the future or another planet or galaxy; story details contain researched scientific facts; the problem the characters face seems logical; the way the problem is resolved seems possible.
6. The characters seem like typical kids looking for adventure; the story takes place on Earth and Mars; someday people could use space scooters of some kind; people are fascinated with finding aliens and visiting Mars.

Tom Thumb: Fairy Tale
1. Answers may include: Parents like to share stories they know well; favorite stories often have lessons to be learned; the stories are memorable since the characters are so life-like.
2. Answers may include: *Cinderella, Snow White, Jack and the Beanstalk, Sleeping Beauty,* and *Rapunzel.*
3. Tom let the thieves think he was helping them. He planned to let the thieves help him get inside the gate, and then he warned the farmer of the theft.
4. Answers will vary.
5. Fairy Tale: a fictional story that may have started through oral story tellings before recorded in print; takes place in a pretend place long, long ago; often contains characters that are either good or bad, and good triumphs over evil; usually conveys a moral or lesson; includes fantastical characters or events; often begins with the words "Once upon a time."
6. The story features fictional characters from long ago; Tom Thumb is only the size of a thumb and can ride on the backs of fish; the thieves are bad while Tom is good.

Paul Bunyan and Babe the Blue Ox: Tall Tale
1. It said Paul cut down trees when the United States was a new country, and Paul Bunyan was responsible for creating the Great Lakes.
3. Paul is so big he made forests fall when he was a baby. He can cut down whole forests. He can dig out rivers and canyons.
4. Answers will vary.
5. Tall Tale: the fictional story takes place in the past; the character's physical attributes or strengths are exaggerated; story may contain real facts or places; the actual events in the story could never happen.
6. Paul Bunyan could not really have existed because he was enormous; his strengths are pretend since a real person couldn't have made the Grand Canyon; and the story contains real places, like Maine, Iowa, North Dakota, and South Dakota.